Text and Tagmeme

Open Linguistics Series

The *Open Linguistics* series, to which this book makes a highly significant contribution, is 'open' in two senses. First, it provides an open forum for works associated with any school of linguistics or with none. Linguistics is emerging from a period in which many (but never all) of the most lifely minds in the subject seemed to assume that transformational generative grammar—or at least something fairly closely derived from it—would provide the main theoretical framework for linguistics for the forseeable future. In Kuhn's terms, linguistics appeared to some to have reached the 'paradigm' stage. Reality today is very different. More and more scholars are examining approaches to language that were formerly scorned for not accepting as central the particular set of concerns highlighted in the Chomskian approach, such as Halliday's systemic theory, Lamb's stratificational model and, as in the case of this book, Pike's tagmemics—while others are developing new or partly new theories. The series is open to all approaches, then—including work in the generativist–formalist tradition.

The second sense in which the series is 'open' is that it encourages works that open out 'core' linguistics in various ways: to encompass discourse and the description of natural texts; to explore the relationships between linguistics and its neighbouring disciplines such as psychology, sociology, philosophy, artificial intelligence, and cultural and literary studies; and to apply it in fields such as education and language pathology.

This book is 'open' in many of these ways. It presents the most recent thinking of the major architect of tagmemic theory; its proposals for discourse grammar are as important as those for sentence grammar; and above all it does what has been done for rather few theoretical models: it *demonstrates* the model at work in the explication of extended natural texts.

Open Linguistics Series Editor
Robin P. Fawcett, The Polytechnic of Wales
Modal Expressions in English, Michael R. Perkins
Text and Tagmeme, Kenneth L. Pike and Evelyn G. Pike
The Semiotics of Culture and Language, eds: Robin P. Fawcett, M. A. K. Halliday, S. M. Lamb and A. Makkai.

Text and Tagmeme

Kenneth L. Pike
and
Evelyn G. Pike

ABLEX Publishing Corporation
Norwood, New Jersey 07648

© Kenneth L. Pike and Evelyn G. Pike 1983

First published in the United States in 1983 by
Ablex Publishing Corporation
355 Chestnut Street, Norwood, New Jersey 07648

Library of Congress Cataloging in Publication Data

Pike, Kenneth Lee, 1912–
   Text and tagmeme.

   1. Tagmemics   2. Grammar, comparative and general.
I. Pike, Evelyn G.   II. Title
P160.P54   1983   415   83–16202
ISBN 0–89391–210–7

Printed in Great Britain

Contents

Class labels are in capital letters.

List of Displays

Acknowledgements

We acknowledge, with appreciation, permission from *The Reader's Digest* to use an excerpt from 'A Question of Honor' by Alan Sherman, *The Reader's Digest*, May 1971.

The selection 'Who But the Lord?' is copyright 1948 by Alfred A. Knopf, Inc. Reprinted from *Selected Poems of Langston Hughes* by Langston Hughes, by permission of the publisher.

Foreword

Kenneth Pike is a remarkable man. Let me mention just four of the many ways in which he is remarkable. The first is for his contributions to not one but several aspects of linguistic theory. *Phonemics* (1947) was a major contribution to phonology; the massive *Language in Relation to a Unified Theory of Human Behaviour* (1954, 1955, 1960; 1967) was perhaps a work that was too far ahead of its time (which was an intensely formalistic time), and the simply written *Linguistic Concepts: An Introduction to Tagmemics* (1982) presents a brief outline of his current thinking about the overall model. And he has also contributed to grammatical theory, *Grammatical Analysis* (1977; 1982) being perhaps the clearest exposition of his proposals. Second, he is a great describer of languages and solver of those practical problems that always arise in any attempt to make a reasonably full description of a natural language. (In passing, we might note that the capacity to generate theory that arouses theoretical interest has by no means always been supported by the capacity to make illuminating and holistic descriptions of real languages, as in Pike's case.) Third, and very closely related to the second, he has been a major driving force in the success of the Summer Institute of Linguistics—an organization with centres in most continents devoted to describing hitherto undescribed languages, devising appropriate writing systems, and then translating the Bible into those languages. (There is also much supporting educational work, in the broadest sense, so that it could be claimed that the SIL plays a valuable role in easing isolated peoples into the twentieth century.) SIL linguists have described over 650 languages, generally in a broadly tagmemic framework. Fourth, Kenneth Pike has immense personal and interpersonal gifts, both as a teacher (and one who knows when it is right to give free rein to the showman in himself!) and as a helper to individuals with problems of every kind, from the linguistic to the personal. His positive, generous and, at 71, still youthful approach to life are clearly not unrelated to his strong Christian commitment.

It has taken a remarkable woman to keep up with this remarkable man. And it is no accident that the main tagmemic handbook on practical descriptive linguistics—*Grammatical Analysis*, mentioned above—is co-authored, like the present book, by his wife Evelyn. But Evelyn's contribution has not only been pedagogical; as the Preface to that book explains (p. xiv): 'Evelyn provided the essential breakthrough to the referential hierarchy'—which, with the grammatical and phonological hierarchies, is one of the three 'levels' or 'strata' (as other theories term them) that are needed for the full explication of a text.

Because of its goal of bible translation, much of the SIL's work has been on languages other than English. This has been at once the strength and the weakness of tagmemics: its strength because it has been tested on as wide a range of languages as one could wish (and certainly more than any other theory), and its weakness because so little of the work has been published, with the result that its strengths are underappreciated by those outside the broad family of SIL linguists. *Grammatical analysis*, however, has frequent examples from English as well as other languages, and the present book, which illustrates the most complete application to date of the concepts associated with the three hierarchies in an exhaustive explication of two English texts, completes the emergence of tagmemics into the public arena. I say this because it is only when a theory is demonstrated at work in extended description of a language which one is at home in that one can truly appreciate it, evaluate it, and compare its ways of solving problems with those that other theories would use. And, since English is the world's most widely used and widely studied language, it is the vital testing grounds of theories. One of the major problems facing linguists today is to work out just how the various theories such as stratificational, systemic, functional and tagmemic grammar relate to each other. This book makes a vital contribution to this goal.

But the book also contains, in Chapter 3, new theory. Kenneth Pike has always been fascinated by the potential for concepts from other disciplines to be relevant to linguistics. For many years the notions of 'field', 'wave' and 'particle' from physics have played a part in his thinking; here he draws on geometry and explains the insights that he has gained from a variety of models, culminating here in the tetrahedron. A tetrahedron is a solid with just four sides, and Pike has a lot of fun exploring the insights to be gained from relating this fact in various ways to the four-cell tagmeme that lies at the heart of tagmemic theory. For those who attended the Ninth International Systemic Workshop in Toronto in 1982 reading Chapter 3 will recall the dramatic presentation which displayed the entertainer in Pike at its very best—and for those who were not, it may be helpful to say that Chapter 3 should be read as a dramatic monologue.

Perhaps the most important thing about Ken's linguistics is not his outstanding scholarship but the fact that he combines this with *enjoying* his linguistics.

The Polytechnic of Wales
July 1983

Robin P. Fawcett

Introduction

We bring to the writing of *Text and Tagmeme* various principles which the reader might like to be aware of since they affect our presentation substantially.

(1) *Life requires context*; autonomy is death. The relevance of a sentence, for example, can be known adequately only if we know the relation of that sentence to the conversation or text within which it occurs. Is it intended as truth, or is it a deliberate lie? For seriousness, or for irony? As a precise statement, or as an elegant recognized hyperbole? As an exercise in logic, or as part of a poem? The 'life' of a sentence involves its impact as intended by its speaker, and the load of information it carries across a communication gap. When the intent is lost by the lack of suitable context, the sentence is 'dead' to its purposes.

In tagmemic theory, of the variety given here, context is shown in terms of units within units, arranged in hierarchical levels. Large units contain smaller ones; smaller ones can be seen as grouped into sub-units of larger ones. These units are not all limited to the sentence or below, but extend upwards to discourses and conversations— which in turn are embedded in still larger units of nonverbal behavior. The emphasis on context has led to calling the tagmeme itself a kind of unit which is a 'unit-in-context.'

(2) But such units with their contexts comprise patterns. And the *presentation* of such an inclusive *pattern* is then a *variety of theory*. An adequate description must, as we have implied above, include an adequate relating of material to its context. But once adequate context (left undefined here) is presented, it will show a pattern of materials, data, relations, observers. Such a contextualized description is itself a variety of theory.

(3) *Person is more important than thing*. Speaker and hearer with their feelings and intents and interpretations and capacities have crucial relevance to language beyond that of abstract classes of items, or rules, or patterns. In language analysis, therefore, we must *somewhere* in our descriptions indicate places that these factors affect the concrete expressions of language. We must find a way to describe and symbolize expressed relations among the observers (speaker, hearer, onlookers, and analyst) and the data.

And the observer is given prominence by an insistence on emic
analysis and description. He has the ability to choose to adopt a
static view of a situation, or a dynamic one, or a relational one—
views which can in turn be seen as involving views of particle, wave,
and field.

(4) Explanation involves truth, *truth involves the relation of units
to patterns*, and pattern involves the *integration* of *data* and of
observer within a larger system. Explanation in isolation is therefore
invalid. Truth is more than abstract theory. It involves description of
detail in relation to a containing system. A theory is useful precisely
because it opens the door to further work through observations and
descriptions, and to further hypotheses related to the pattern already
observed and presented.

These, and other principles of tagmemic theory, underlie Pike
(1967). And in Pike and Pike (1982) we show in detail how grammatical analysis using these principles can be taught in the classroom
with detailed exercises. In this present volume, however, we have a
different aim. In Chapter 1 Evelyn Pike gives the exegesis of a short
text, 'The Bathtub Navy,' which shows its grammatical and referential patterns. The reader should try to give prime attention to the
displays in it, rather than to the discussion as such. It is in the
displays that the practical and theoretical viewpoint can best be seen;
the verbal description is aimed at helping the reader to be able to
understand the details of these displays. This analysis is more complete than any other we have done thus far.

In Chapter 2, Kenneth Pike gives a comparable analysis of the
phonology of a poem—our only extensive treatment of the four-
cell hierarchical phonology of a text. Thus the basic tagmemic
universals of human behavior find extended application to the
phonological area, and continue to give promise of being fruitful
not only for linguistics proper, but also for sociolinguistics, psycho-
linguistics, semiotics, and anthropology. Then, in Chapter 3, Kenneth
Pike presents a geometric model of the tagmeme itself. In this
model certain central contrastive features may at first appear as
irregular in relation to a low-level structure, but later appear as
regular in relation to a higher level structure as modelled by a
tetrahedron.

This book, then, contains our latest and most extensive application of tagmemic theory to the analysis of texts. It does so in hierarchical levels of grammar, of reference, and of phonology. And it
shows how irregularities—residues—in a description may hide clues
to major theoretical advances in understanding human behavior. It
illustrates how reductionism can be fatal to a fuller measure of

understanding of structural behavior, since high-level structures may carry their own patterns which are not deducible from low-level ones.

1 Grammatical and Referential Hierarchies in a Prose Text— Toward its Systematic Exegesis

Evelyn G. Pike

1.0 TOWARD THE UNDERSTANDING OF A STREAM OF SPEECH

Some essential factors contributing to the understanding of a stream of speech comprise the topic of this study. What is a systematic way of exegeting a text? The author used the following text of thirteen sentences to illustrate the form-meaning units by which she has understood the text, 'The Bathtub Navy,' frequently identified in this chapter as BN (see Display 1.1).

The first part of the chapter (1.1) presents a sketch of the tag-memic model. The rest concerns the text itself: (1.2) analyzes its grammar, (1.3) its reference, (1.4) something of the greater lexicon, and (1.5) gives a summary.

The grammatical and referential analysis is presented in displays of tree diagrams and formulas. The tree diagrams show more directly the hierarchical relation of constituent to constituent. That information is then transposed into formulas. Cohesion features have been added to the grammatical formulas, and slot, role, as well as cohesion, to referential formulas. Formulas are generalizations for each contrastive construction, potentially accounting for all variants occurring in BN. Due to lack of time and space, however, some constructions and variants have been omitted; for example, only two sentences have been included in this analysis, and these are developed down to morpheme (however, I have not listed morpheme classes). These lower grammatical structures are not the primary concern of this paper; such structures have been discussed extensively in Pike and Pike (1982).

Each constituent is identified by number both in the tree diagrams and the formulas. Grammatical constituents are prefaced by GC, and referential constituents are prefaced by RC. Constituents whose numbers begin with 0 are those of the speaker-hearer structure; other numbers are of the text itself. The referential substance of the text is the list of events to which the text refers. These are numbered in chronological order and prefaced by RE (Referential Event); see Display 1.12. These events are to the referential structure approximately what sentences are to the grammatical structure.

Display 1.1 'The Bathtub Navy' (BN) (a selection from 'A Question of Honour' by Allan Sherman in *Reader's Digest*, Vol. 98, No. 589, May 1971: 77–78)

(G1.1) On May 26, 1940, (G1.2) as Hitler's armies overran France, (G1.3) British and French troops retreated by the tens of thousands into the little French port of Dunkirk. (G2) From Dunkirk there was no place left to go but into the English Channel.

(G3) The mighty British navy had few ships small enough or agile enough to go in and evacuate the men. (G4.1) Thus the Free World could do nothing but sit by the radio in frustration and anguish, (G4.2) waiting for news that these vast armies of brave men had been wiped out.

(G5.1) Then (G5.2) in the early hours of May 27, (G5.3) a miracle began to unfold. (G6.1) From everywhere in the British Isles they came—(G6.2) poor fishermen with creaky, (G6.3) beat-up fishing boats, (G6.4) noblemen with yachts, (G6.5) sportsmen with racing yawls and motor launches. (G7.1) The first of this motley fleet, (G7.2) captained by men with neither guns nor uniforms, (G7.3) set sail by moonlight from Sheerness, (G7.4) putt-putting across U-boat-and-mine-infested water. (G8.1) As the morning sun lighted the beaches of Dunkirk, (G8.2) the first of the hundreds of small boats pulled onto the shore. (G9.1) The cheers of the trapped soldiers were drowned out by the roar of the Luftwaffe overhead, (G9.2) strafing and bombing the beach, (G9.3) and by the crackle of British Spitfires trying to fight them off.

(G10.1) Under that hell in the sky, (G10.2) the miracle of Dunkirk continued for nine days and nights. (G11.1) All together, (G11.2) 338,226 British and French lives were saved.

(G12.1) On June 18, (G12.2) Winston Churchill said, (G12.3) 'Let us therefore brace ourselves to our duties and so bear ourselves that, (G12.4) if the British Empire and its Commonwealth last for a thousand years, (G12.5) men will still say: (G12.6) '*This was their finest hour.*'

(G13.1) For the men of His Majesty's Bathtub Navy, (G13.2) the finest hour of all (G13.3)—the hour of greatest honor (G13.4)—took place on the beaches at Dunkirk.

Note: The author has added numbers to the text for identification. The first number indicates the sentence and the second a part of the sentence. When referring to these sentences the number will be prefaced by G, meaning grammatical sentence.

1.1 THE TAGMEMIC MODEL: THE HIERARCHIES

1.1.1 Their content

The tagmemic model of communication considers each stream of speech to exhibit three simultaneous structures: phonology, grammar, and reference. Phonology has to do with sound structure: phonemes, syllables, stress and pause groups, pitch, and voice quality, among other things. This chapter does not treat that structure, but it may be seen in Chapter 2. Grammar has to do with morphemes, words, phrases, sentences, conversation. Reference has to do with what a stream of speech refers to—what it is talking about. It refers to qualities, identities, events, and purposeful sequences of events which make up the total macro-event. If these events were historical they could have been photographed, or if imaginary could have been drawn; in both instances they can be talked about.

This is consonant with a statement in Miller and Johnson-Laird (1976: 6) 'If linguistic communication is to be of any practical value, words must not only be related to one another through grammatical, conceptual, or memorial systems; they must also be related to what is 'out there,' to what people want to talk about, to the things and events people perceive around them.' Our referential hierarchy concerns the organization of that 'out there' which is being talked about.

The decoding of a stream of speech involves understanding the phonology, grammar, and reference. In order to gain that understanding, we elicit metatexts which all of us use informally to understand one another from day to day. Phonologically if a sound is in question: *Did you say Ella or Ethel*? For grammatical role: *Did you mean that he did it because . . . or did he just happen to*? Referential sequence and identity: *Did he arrive before or after you did*? Or: *Who was it that gave the money*? Such questions are essential to our everyday understanding of one another. Here, we have provided a way of using metatext for decoding a stream of speech. The interest of the decoder determines the kinds of metatext he needs for his purposes. The more diverse the structures of the speaker and hearer, the more extensive the metatexts must be.

1.1.2 Their levels of structure

These structures are hierarchical in that each unit occurs in a larger structure (context) and conversely every construction is made up of a sequence of units. These three hierarchies show part-whole relations rather than the generic-specific relations of a taxonomic hierarchy, or one of ranking of features such as that in Foley and Van Valin (1977) in their ranking of referential features.

Each immediate part of a whole is an immediate constituent of that whole. If a constituent has no inner parts (phonological for phonology, grammatical for grammar, referential for reference), then it is a minimal unit. All other units are constructions and have at least two immediate constituents. We assume that, except for the repetition of the same unit, there will be no more than about seven immediate constituents in a construction. We base this on Miller's

(1956) 'magical number seven.' We assume that part-whole relations are essential as implied by this constraint on human perception.

Tagmemics is careful to observe hierarchical levels and describe each unit in respect to those levels. Each unit at each level of each hierarchy has its contrastive-identificational features, which include all variants of the unit. Formulas exhibit those features and variants, as well as identifying the distributional features of each unit. For a beginning etics of grammatical levels we draw on the paired hierarchy as described in Pike and Pike (1982: 23, Display 2). The longer the text, the more layerings there will be, hence the problem arises as to which groupings are separate level types in contrast to recursion of units of the same structural level. Since this indeterminacy is not a major concern of this paper, we merely present some of the grammatical levels we have posited for BN: speaker-hearer axis, monolog, section, paragraph cluster, paragraph, sentence cluster, sentence, clause, clause root, phrase, word, morpheme cluster, and morpheme.

Display 1.2 Chart of Paired Grammatical Levels

Meaning	Minimum Unit	Expanded Unit
Social Interaction	Exchange	Conversation
Theme-Development	Paragraph/Sentence Cluster	Monolog
Proposition	Clause	Sentence
Term	Word	Phrase
Lexical Package	Morpheme	Morpheme Cluster

These are structures posited specifically for English; other languages may exhibit more levels between some of these English levels, or may not show contrast between other English levels. Although the presence of levels of structure is a universal, the specific kinds and number of contrastive levels is language specific, and in a particular level may vary some with the discourse type—e.g. the addition of chapters to a book in English.

For the referential hierarchy of BN (historical report) we posit the following levels: performative interaction, macro-event, vector, complex, event, identity, and relation. More study in respect to referential levels needs to be done, but at least these are required for this text and for others which we have studied.

We find very interesting parallels between the levels of the hierarchies relative to independency-dependency: for grammar between clause and phrase; for reference between event and identity; for phonology between stress group and syllable. Between each of these pairs is a major threshold. Grammatical phrases and words label terms whereas clauses and sentences relate terms to each other as propositions, hence are much more independent than are phrases and words. Analogously events relate identities to each other to form a purposeful action or happening, hence are more independent than an identity (entity). Relations are still more dependent than identities in that they require more than one part. Some of them require two parts while others require three parts. Consider the three-part relation of *on* which requires two other parts to know its meaning: *book* (entity) *on* (relation) *table* (entity). This is somewhat analogous to the bound nature of affixes in grammar.

1.1.3 The tagmeme: unit-in-context

Each immediate constituent in each level of each of the three hierarchies represents (or manifests) a tagmeme. A tagmeme is characterized by four features. They are contrastive-identificational features. These may be presented in a four-cell display, any three of which

Display 1.3 Contrastive Features of the Tagmeme

Slot	Class(es)
(Where?)	(What?)
Role	Cohesion
(Why?)	(How governs/ is governed?)

have something in common in contrast to the fourth. (a) *Class* is substance, that which is seen or heard directly, whereas the other three relate to the context hence the source of the term unit-in-context. (b) *Slot* has to do with the place and prominence of the substance in the immediately larger structure, whereas the other three are the distinctive characteristics of that place. (c) *Role* is function, or grammatical meaning, referred to by some linguists as a part of deep structure or as pragmatics, whereas the other three have to do with form. (d) *Cohesion* includes relations to the larger context, whereas the other three have to do only with the immediate context.

To identify each of these features, typical questions need to be asked. (a) For *class* we ask: What? What part of the stream of speech is being considered? What part can be replaced with a second stream of speech and retain the same relation to the context? An example: *He saw the boy, He saw two little girls*, and *He saw them*. The replaceable parts are *the boy, two little girls*, and *them*. The first two are noun phrases whereas *them* is a pronoun; all three make up a filler class and as such is the prime means of classification. The differentiation within a grammatical filler class has largely to do with differences of internal structure. (b) For *slot* we ask: Where? In which immediately larger including structure does the class occur and with what relative prominence in relation to the other immediate constituents of that including structure? An example: Noun phrase is the immediately larger structure in which *boy* occurs; *the boy* has prominence there, hence fills the slot of nucleus of the noun phrase; *the* fills a marginal slot of the noun phrase. (c) For *role* we ask: Why? Why does it occur? What does it do? What function does the class have in relation to the other immediate constituents of the including structure? Examples: *the* in the noun phrase *the boy* fills the role of specificity, and *boy* fills the role of item. In *The boy is big* the whole noun phrase fills the slot of subject of the clause root, and also has the role of item. We say that these two different tagmemes, noun phrase nucleus and the subject of a clause root, have the same role; they have the function of itemizing something. More examples of role: *The wind was blowing hard so he didn't play badminton* in which the first clause has the role of cause in relation to the effect role of the second clause. The roles are the same for the following two clauses: *Because the wind was blowing hard he didn't play badminton*. (d) For *cohesion* we ask: Whence? What governs or controls the occurrence of the tagmeme or the occurrence of any particular member of the class in relation to the occurrence of a particular member of a class in another tagmeme, whether large or small? These questions are relevant for all three hierarchies. An example regarding the control of the occurrence of a grammatical tagmeme: Consider the noun phrases *big boys, the boy*, and *one boy* in the sentences *Big boys eat a lot, The boy eats a lot*, and *One boy doesn't eat much*. If the noun is singular, either the tagmeme represented by *the* or the one represented by *one* must occur, otherwise both are optional. Thus the number of the noun controls or governs the occurrence of one or the other of those two tagmemes. An example regarding the control or government of the co-occurrence of one member of a class with another: *Tomorrow he will talk to them* and *Yesterday he was talking to them,* in which *tomorrow* and *yesterday* are members of the same class, but one requires future time in the verb phrase whereas the other requires past time.

It may be pointed out that class is usually viewed as a particle, whereas slot more easily speaks to the wave nature of the tagmeme by designating the peak or margin of the wave of speech. On the other hand cohesion brings in the relation of the unit to the whole field structure of a stream of speech. It is that nature which delays the recognition of many cohesion features, because many streams of speech must sometimes be studied in order to recognize those field relations. Almost any type of cohesion is a worthy topic for considerable study, but in this paper we only hint at the most obvious cohesion features.

Tagmemes in the grammatical formulas are presented in the order in which they are spoken. Tagmemes in referential formulas are presented in the chronological order of events; for lower levels, initiators of action precede action; relations occur adjacent to entities being related.

1.1.4 The usefulness of the model

We have found this model comprehensive, coherent, insightful and viable. It provides a metalanguage for treating a vast amount of communication data in a coherent fashion, asking essentially the same questions of each unit. The tagmeme is a relatively simple concept. The number of tagmemes is vast and allows for newly developing units representing an expanding culture. Tagmemic hierarchical organization allows for relatively simple retrieval of information and gives stability to the analysis in that complexity is distributed over different hierarchies and different levels of those hierarchies, and also over different observer involvements. New information and minor irregularities can be encapsulated in a hierarchical level without basic upset of other levels.

This model is applicable to masses of natural language data and is teachable—including at beginning levels. It allows one to begin work on any level, proceding either up or down in any of the hierarchies. The core of a selected study can be relatively well defined, whereas the context of that core fades out of attention to the extent that the more remote contexts have no need of mention at all. The depth of analysis to which one goes is dependent on the observer-analyst. If he is an acoustician he will go lower in the phonological structure than a literacy specialist. If he is an atomic physicist, he'll elicit more text in order to go lower in the referential structure than do we who are interested only in the understanding of what Sherman has to say about the bathtub navy. The atomic physicist is interested in the molecular and atomic nature of the steel in those U-boats; we aren't. We finish with our description when we think we have understood what the speaker/author has said and when we can paraphrase it in such a way that we think he will say that we have understood him. Understanding is, from this perspective, something of an implicit cross-cultural paraphrase which can in turn be viewed as a kind of translation. This process involves the structure of all three hierarchies. The hearer, in decoding a stream of speech, brings to bear his phonological idiolect, and his grammatical idiolect, as well as his referential idiolect—his world view and notions of his culture. The more that these structures of the encoder and the decoder are alike, the greater and more immediate is the understanding.

1.2 THE GRAMMATICAL STRUCTURE OF 'THE BATHTUB NAVY' (BN)

1.2.1 The segmentation of REPORT MONOLOG (BN) down to sentence

There are three major parts or constituents in the report, each of which is introduced by a sentence with a date margin: (1) *on May 26, 1940*, (2) *in the early hours of May 27*, and (3) *on June 18*. This would at first suggest that the three are immediate constituents of the report; however, the second part is introduced by the sentence-sequence word *then* which indicates that the second is more closely related to the first than it is to the third. Also, in the first two parts verbs of action plus their actors are prevalent, whereas in the third part there are only comments relevant to the actions. In those comments, summary terms such as *therefore* in *therefore let us . . .* and *this* in *This was their finest hour* in the quotation from Churchill refer to all that is mentioned in the preceding paragraphs. *His Majesty's Bathtub Navy* in G13.1 is a summary term for the men and equipment which are listed in G6.2-5. The term *the finest hour of all —the hour of greatest honor* summarizes what is stated in some detail in G5-10. This supports the unity of the third part in contrast to the first two parts. Thus instead of three immediate constituents

Display 1.4A Grammatical Tree Diagram of REPORT MONOLOG (BN) Developed Down to Sentence

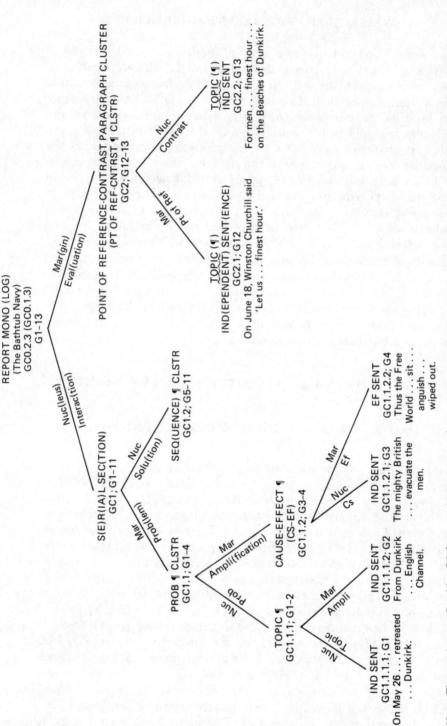

Note: The numbers prefixed by GC (grammatical constituent) identify each grammatical constituent on the tree; the numbers prefixed by G (grammatical sentence) identify a specific sentence or sentence part in the discourse. The numbers are used for reference especially in the formulas. Features of cohesion are included only in the formulas.

Display 1.4B Grammatical Tree Diagram of REPORT MONOLOG (BN) Developed Down to Sentence (Continued)

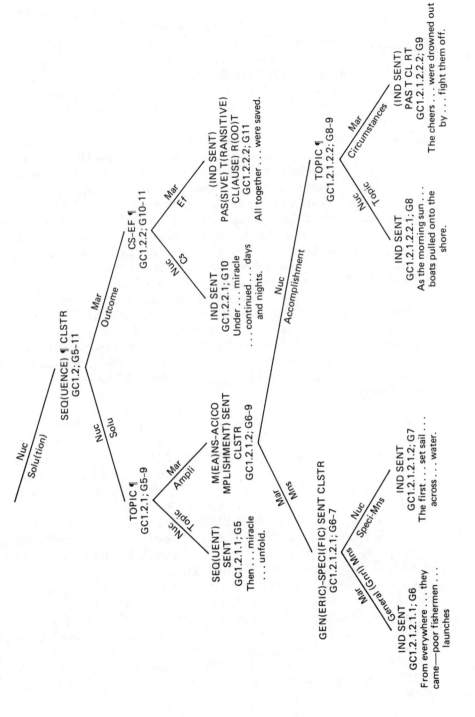

in the REPORT MONOLOG (R MONO) there are just two. The first two parts form the unit SERIAL SECTION (SRL SEC) GC1; G1–11, which fills the nucleus of R MONO, having the role of interaction. Then the third part, POINT OF REFERENCE-CONTRAST PARA–GRAPH CLUSTER (PT OF REF-CNRST ¶ CLSTR) GC2; G12–13, is the second immediate constituent of R MONO filling the margin with the role of evaluation.

It is in Displays 1.4A and 1.4B that our successive segmentation of BN down to sentence is most easily seen. The class label appears at the node and has its constituent number prefaced by GC; its place in the BN text is prefaced by G. Each branch from a node represents an immediate constituent of the class at that node. The slot label of the immediate constituent occurs above the branch and its role label below the branch. The class filling that slot-role is at the end of the branch; each such branch represents a tagmeme. Each label is written in full at its first appearance on the chart from left to right and top to bottom; the abbreviation is the part not in parentheses or is in parentheses beneath the full form. Occasionally a class label totally enclosed in parentheses appears above a second class label. The first class of the two is the more normally expected filler of the given slot-role, but in the given instance only the nucleus of that construction occurs, hence the second label is that of the class filling that nuclear slot and the immediate constituents from that node are those of the second listed class.

The SRL SEC has two immediate constituents—the first two above-mentioned parts marked by dates. The first is PROBLEM PARAGRAPH CLUSTER (PROB ¶ CLSTR) GC1.1; G1–4 and the second is SEQUENCE (SEQ) ¶ CLSTR GC1.2; G5–11; the first is marginal to the second. The internal structure of these two constructions is very similar in that they have an identical sequence of classes: TOPIC ¶ and CAUSE-EFFECT (CS-EF) ¶. However the slots and roles which those paragraphs fill differ; the slot-role filled by the first TOPIC ¶ is nucleus of PROB ¶ CLSTR with the role of problem, whereas the slot-role filled by the second TOPIC ¶ is nucleus of SEQ ¶ CLSTR with the role of solution. Here, as is often the case, the nucleus of a construction has the same role as its including structure. Similarly, the two examples of CS-EF ¶ fill different slot-roles: the roles of amplification and outcome, respectively. These are examples which show that slot, class, and role are independent variables: a class may fill several different slot-roles. In the next paragraph we show that more than one class fills a single slot-role in BN. See GC1.1.2, G3–4 in Display 1.4A and GC1.2.2, G10–11 in Display 1.4B.

Only the first example of CS-EF ¶ is marked for either cause or effect; none the less that pragmatic impact is also present in the second example. The sentence-effect word *thus* in G4 introduces the effect that the Free World is expecting imminent destruction of the troops from the cause that the navy hasn't enough ships. The second example, without overt marking, is G10–11 in which the miracle of Dunkirk is the cause of saving many lives. We could expect that a paraphrase including an overt cause or effect marker would be accepted as capturing the meaning intended. We find these examples comparable to the marked versus unmarked lower level forms in: *then, it rained, so the children came into the house* versus *then, it rained; the children came into the house.* In actual conversation, the roles of the kind seen in the latter example are sometimes verified by asking the question: *Do you mean that the children came in because it rained*? Returning to the BN examples, note that the sentence introduced by *thus* is an effect sentence GC1.1.2.2 having an effect role, whereas only the nucleus of an independent sentence has the effect role in the second example. In Display 1.10, Formula 10, the two classes are both shown to fill the margin-effect of the CS-EF ¶. An additional example of an effect sentence in the quotation by Churchill, marked by the effect word *therefore*, Display 1.6, GC2.1.2b.3.1.

We have posited a third example of a topic paragraph in which the small boats pull on to shore as the battle continues: GC1.2.1.2.2; G8–9. The independent sentence, about the boats, fills the nucleus-topic slot-role, but the second sentence, about the cheers being drowned out by the continuing battle, we see as filling a margin-circumstance. The margin in the other two topic paragraphs has the role of amplification. We are assuming, however, that both a margin-amplification and a margin-circumstance can occur in a topic paragraph, and are both optional, but we just do not have such an example in BN.

Another construction whose role we have deduced, and which we would expect to be verified elsewhere or by an overtly marked paraphrase, is the PT OF REF-CONTRST ¶ CLSTR G12–13. Churchill's statement about Britain's finest hour is the point of reference against which Sherman presents the contrast for BN's finest hour. For meaning purposes—not style—we would expect that *however* could have introduced Sentence 13 concerning the Bathtub Navy's finest hour. We concur with the author's judgement in considering the two constituent parts as paragraphs—parallel with the two other date marked parts—each with two paragraphs. But these latter two paragraphs have just one sentence each filling the nuclear slot, with no paragraph margin. These might be one of a number of different kinds of paragraphs, but as an initial guess we would suggest topic paragraph as being the most useful. This is indicated by our wavy line under TOPIC for GC2.1 and GC2.2 in Display 1.4A and Display 1.10, Formula 8.

We are interested in the fact that the two paragraphs mentioned above are closely related not only by being in the single date part, but also by their being tied lexically by *finest hour* in each of them, G12.6 and G13.2. Such lexical repetitions show relatedness of grammatical parts. Note the use of *miracle* to tie together the two middle paragraphs in *miracle began to unfold* G5.3 and *miracle . . . continued for nine days . . .* G10.2. Then that latter use of *miracle* gives prominence to G10 in contrast to G11 which states the number of lives saved. Another lexical tie is seen between G1 and G2: *. . . into the little French port of Dunkirk*, and *From Dunkirk . . .* A further lexical tie is with the word *honor*. It occurs in the last sentence of BN, tying the whole text to the title of the *Reader's Digest* article entitled 'A Question of Honor.' Other sections of the article are likewise about honor, hence BN is tied in with them as well.

There are two examples in Display 1.4A of constructions smaller than a paragraph and larger than a sentence: a sentence cluster. The M(EA)NS-AC(OMPLISHMENT) SENT(ENCE) CLUSTER (CLSTR) GC1.2.1.2; G6–9 Display 1.4B has a margin-means filled by the embedded GEN(ERIC)-SPECI(FIC) SENT CLSTR followed by nucleus-accomplishment filled by the embedded TOPIC ¶ GC1.2.1.2.2; G8–9 which we have discussed above, the one whose margin is circumstance rather than amplification. The GEN-SPECI SENT CLSTR in turn has a margin-general means followed by a nucleus-specific means. Each of these is filled by an independent sentence. In Displays 1.4A and 1.4B the grammatical structure of BN is developed down to sentence or to a lower level manifesting a sentence. Note that the depth of layering is indicated by the number of digits in the GC number. The Sentences 6–9 within this part each have six numbers. Those preceding them (G1–5) and two following them (G10–11) have four numbers. However the last two sentences (G12–13) have only two GC digits.

1.2.2 Degrees of nuclearity and marginality

You have seen in this text that we have needed to use only two degrees of prominence: nucleus and margin. That does not preclude the usefulness, however, of more degrees for other texts. Nevertheless, with just two degrees combined with constituent layering, multiple degrees of nuclearity and marginality are indicated. Following from the top of Display 1.4A and on into the Display 1.4B, the four successive nuclei, we have Sentence 5, the unfolding of a miracle, as the only sentence in BN which is a part of nuclei exclusively; it is the topic sentence of the whole discourse. The roles within which it occurs (topic, then solution, solution, interaction) show that it is the topic of the solution within interaction. Now consider the part which is marginal to that topic sentence and which fills the margin-amplification G6–9. Follow down through the nuclei of that part and you find Sentence 8 *As the morning sun . . . boats pulled onto the shore.* It is this sentence which presents how the solution is to be accomplished. Note that its immediate role is topic, then accomplishment, then amplification of the topic role, both of which occur within the role of solution and ultimately of interaction. Thus, adding the successive layerings of role to those of slot, a great deal of information can be indicated concerning the importance, or grammatical prominence and function, which each part has to other parts.

1.2.3 Sentence structure

We present the analysis of just two sentences: G1 and G12. The tree diagram for the first sentence is in Displays 1.5A and 1.5B and its formulas are in Display 1.11. The higher levels of G12 are presented in the tree-network diagram in Display 1.6 and the lower levels in Display 1.7; there are no formulas for these constructions.

The structure of Sentence 12 is of some interest to us here. The identification of the speaker and addressee is a normal artifact of narrative discourse (but not of drama). We consider the quotation as nuclear to the discourse, whereas the identification of speaker and addressee is marginal. This is indicated by the two constituents of the class I-THOU-HERE-NOW AXIS GC2.1.2a (all of G12 except the date). *Winston Churchill said* is SPEECH FRAGMENT GC2.1.2a.1 which is margin-speech setting, whereas the quotation is DIRECT QUOTATION MONOLOG manifested by only its nuclear element: EFFECT SENT GC2.1.2a.2. Because it is at this reported speech level only that the sequence *Winston Churchill said* fills just one slot, and because we want to show its similarity of structure to *Winston Churchill wanted coffee*, we then join the branches of the tree to form a network in the class ENCODING BITRANSITIVE CLAUSE ROOT GC2.1.2b and develop that structure as we do other clause roots. The *b* in the GC number indicates a lower level analysis which differs from its structure at a higher level. Each quotation is an example of the I-THOU-HERE-NOW AXIS, whose parts may be

Display 1.5A Grammatical Tree Diagram of Sentence 1

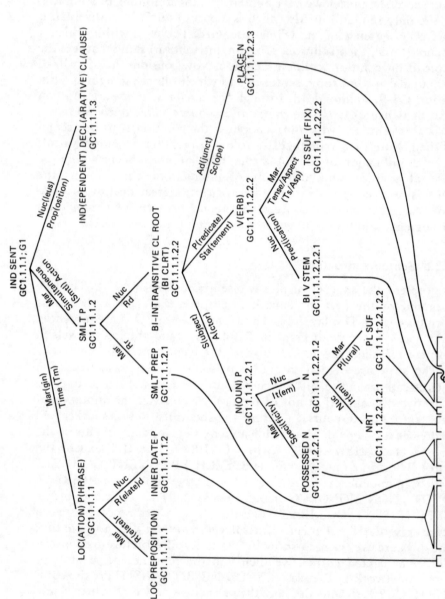

Display 1.5B Grammatical Tree Diagram of Sentence 1 (Continued)

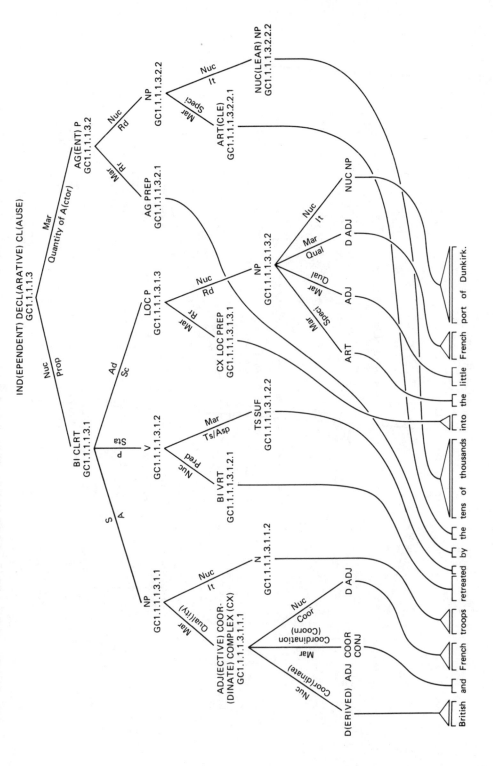

Display 1.6 Grammatical Tree Diagram of the Higher Levels of Sentence 12

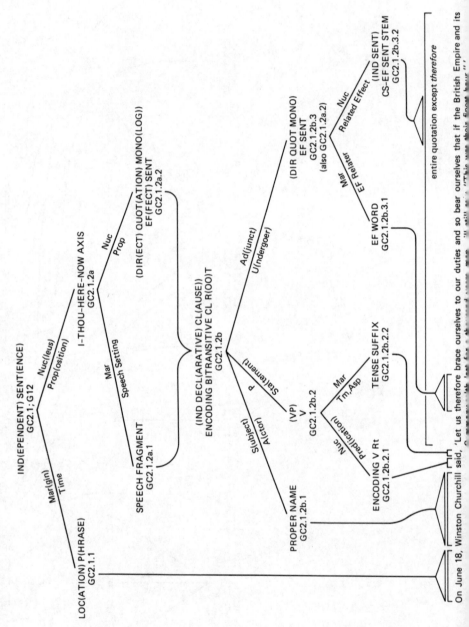

On June 18, Winston Churchill said, 'Let us therefore brace ourselves to our duties and so bear ourselves that if the British Empire and its

either explicit or only implicit. The decoding part is much less frequently explicit than parts of the encoding constituent. Note that the quotation EFFECT SENT is GC2.1.2a.2 as the higher level constituent of the axis, but is GC2.1.2b.3 as the lower level constituent in the clause root—the stream of speech is identical for both.

Note that the sentence-effect word *therefore* does not occur at the beginning of the sentence but rather interrupts the second constituent which is a CAUSE-EFFECT SENT STEM GC2.1.2b.3.2.

In Display 1.7 we see that the effect of the cause of 'bracing ourselves . . .' is to be found in multiple layers of roles: effect, related purpose, and contingency which is filled by another embedded ENCODING BITRANSITIVE CLAUSE ROOT GC2.1.2b.3.2.2.2.2 *men will still say: 'This was their finest hour.'* Also note that the PURPOSE PHRASE GC2.1.2b.3.2.2.1 *so . . . that* has discontinuous constituents, and as a unit is marginal to the PURPOSE SENT.

1.2.4 The I-THOU-HERE-NOW AXIS

There is a speaker–hearer relation either implicit or explicit for every stream of speech. We have chosen to bypass the extra complexity of the writing, publishing and reading of this text by considering the text to have been told to the authors by Allan Sherman. That relation between Sherman and the authors is implicit and may be expressed by a communication exchange GC0.1 *I say something to you.* GC0.2 *I hear something from you.* This we have called the I-THOU-HERE-NOW AXIS.

The 'something,' which is a REPORT MONOLOG, is the topic of this paper: how do the authors decode the 'something.' For that reason the authors list the monolog as primarily from the decoding clause root—the GC from the encoding clause root is in parentheses. No attempt has been made here to evaluate how close the decoding product is to the encoding product. That would entail multiple paraphrases and Sherman's responses as to which paraphrases were, indeed, what he meant and which were not.

The first constituent of the axis, ENCODING BITRANSITIVE CLAUSE ROOT, has been discussed above as the direct quotation of Churchill in G12. Some encoding verb roots are *say, reply, answer, ask, request.* The DECODING BITRANSITIVE CLAUSE ROOT is very much less frequently explicit. The tree diagram for this axis is presented in Display 1.8 and the formulas in Display 1.9.

Display 1.7 Grammatical Tree Diagram of Part of the Quotation in Sentence 12 (Continued from Display 1.6)

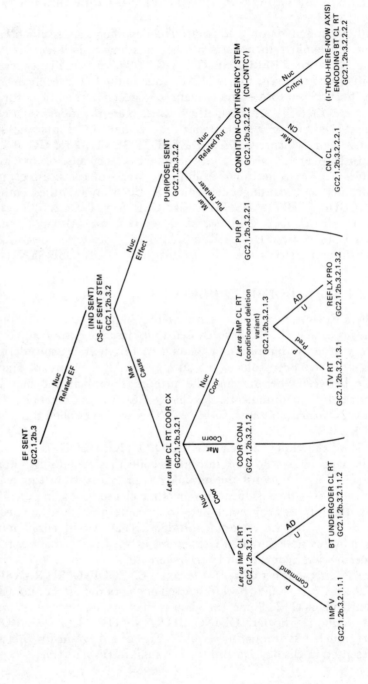

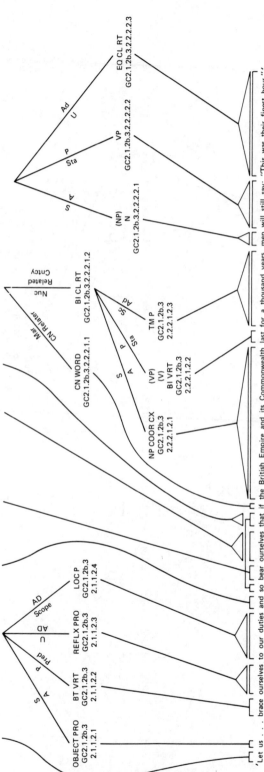

Display 1.8 Grammatical Tree Diagram of Speaker-Hearer Relationship in Space and Time;
the I-THOU-HERE-NOW AXIS which Underlies Every Stream of Speech

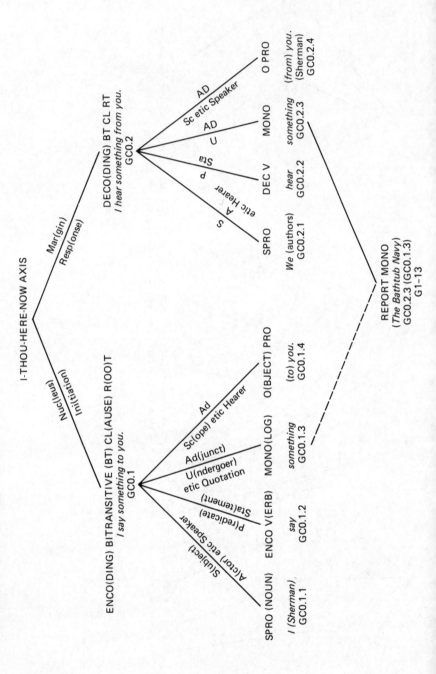

1.2.5 Grammatical cohesion features

Cohesion features have not been indicated in the tree displays, but rather only in the formulas. Some of the most interesting are to be found in the I-THOU-HERE-NOW AXIS. See Display 1.9. The first formula is to be read: I-THOU-HERE-NOW AXIS equals an EN-CODING BITRANSITIVE CLAUSE ROOT filling a slot of nucleus (of AXIS) with the role of initiation, and cohesion of (1) obligatory occurrence, with (2) requirement of same place and time in both nucleus and margin of the axis. It is followed by a DECODING BITRANSITIVE CLAUSE ROOT filling the slot of margin (of AXIS) with the role of response, and cohesion the same as for the preceding tagmeme (GC 0.1). All other formulas are read comparably. If several classes manifest a single tagmeme, each is joined by implicit *or*. For example: NOUN PHRASE or PRONOUN filling a given slot. Both immediate constituents of the axis, encoding and decoding, require the same time and place. Within the encoding clause root, the subject by his personal grammatical and esthetic competences governs the encoding form of MONOLOG. Not just any monolog may occur in the encoding clause root; its grammatical structure is governed by specific characteristics of the speaker. Esthetic features involve the selection from all the possible grammatical forms available to him, just those he considers appropriate for a short historical report. All such features are listed in both the governing tagmeme and the governed tagmeme. Analogously, the decoder's 'personal grammatical and esthetic competences govern the decoding of MONOLOG.'

Another important cohesion feature within a discourse is the coherence of time. The basic or global or story time is the relation of the time of the speaker to the time of the incidents he is refer-ring to. In this instance the narrator is giving an historical report, REPORT MONOLOG, hence the basic time is past. For prophecy it would be future. In this discourse, except within embedded direct quotation, all dates are in past time and all verb margins in which there is a choice of time are in past time. See Displays 1.10 and 1.11. For each embedded quotation there is a new basic time as well as new speaker-hearer relations. There are two of these in BN, one embedded in the other. Churchill uses the nonpast in *let us . . . brace ourselves . . . and so bear ourselves*, and the future in *men will say*. Note that within the quotation the speaker is part of the first person as are the hearers in the forms *us* and *ourselves*. Only past is used in the quotation embedded in Churchill's quotation. This relates to what men in the future will say relative to a former activity.

Display 1.9 Grammatical Formulas for the I-THOU-HERE-NOW AXIS: Formulas 1-3

(1) I-THOU-HERE-NOW AXIS =

Class: ENCODING BITRANSITIVE CLAUSE ROOT
Slot: Nucleus (of AXIS)
Role: Initiation
Cohesion: (1) Obligatory, (2) Requires same place and time in both
nucleus and margin of the axis (time is overt within the verb)
GC0.1 *I say something to you.*

Class: DECODING BITRANSITIVE CLAUSE
Slot: Margin (of AXIS)
Role: Response
Cohesion: Same as for GC0.1
GC0.2 *I hear something from you.*

(2) ENCODING BITRANSITIVE CLAUSE ROOT =

Class: NOUN PHRASE
        SUBJECT PRONOUN
Slot: Subject (of BT ENC CL RT)
Role: Actor
Cohesion: (1) Obligatory and requires first person in a non-embedded
axis, (2) Optional in some other constructions, (3) Personal
grammatical and esthetic competences govern encoding form of
MONOLOG
GC0.1.1 *I* (Sherman)

Class: ENCODING VERB*
Slot: Predicate (of BT ENC CL RT)
Role: Statement
Cohesion: (1) Obligatory, (2) Mutual requirement of ENCODING
VERB with Subject-as-Actor and Adjunct-as-Scope†
GC0.1.2 *say*

Class: (TO)§ OBJECT PRONOUN
Slot: Adjunct
Role: Scope
Cohesion: (1) Obligatory and requires second person in an axis under-
lying a whole discourse, (2) Optional in some constructions
GC0.1.4 *to you* (authors)

Class: REPORT MONOLOG‡ (BN)
Slot: Adjunct (of BT ENC CL RT)
Role: Undergoer
Cohesion: (1) Obligatory, (2) Requires same MONOLOG in both
GC0.1.3 and in GC0.2.3, (3) Is governed by (3) in S-A GC0.1.1,
(4) Historical report governs occurrence of past tense in all
tagmemes with the role of time except within embedded quotation
GC0.1.3 *something* (*The Bathtub Navy*)

(3) DECODING BITRANSITIVE CLAUSE ROOT =

Class: NOUN PHRASE
  SUBJECT PRONOUN
Slot: Subject (of DEC BT CL RT)
Role: Actor
Cohesion: (1) Obligatory and requires first person in a non-embedded
    axis, (2) optional in some other constructions, (3) Personal gram-
    matical and esthetic competences govern decoding of MONOLOG
  GC0.2.1 I /(authors)

Class: DECODING VERB
Slot: Predicate (of DEC BT CL RT)
Role: Statement
Cohesion: (1) Obligatory, (2) Mutual requirement of DECODING
    VERB with Subject-as-Adjunct-as-Undergoer, Adjunct-as-Scope
  GC0.2.2 hear

Class: REPORT MONOLOG (BN)
Slot: Adjunct (of DEC BT CL RT)
Role: Undergoer
Cohesion: (1) Same as (1) and (2) in GC0.1.3, (2) Is governed by (3)
    in S-A, GC0.2.1
  GC0.2.3 something (The Bathtub Navy)

Class: (FROM) § OBJECT PRONOUN
Slot: Adjunct
Role: Scope
Cohesion: Same as for GC0.1.4
  GC0.2.4 from you (Sherman)

* Some other encoding verb roots are: say, report, affirm, think, command, question.
† The mutual requirement of a particular verb root and accompanying clause root tagmemes is a feature of transitivity and is a cohesion feature of
each tagmeme so involved, but by convention we list this cohesion feature only in the predicate tagmeme.
‡ The specific monolog with which this paper is concerned is 'The Bathtub Navy' which is a member of the class REPORT MONOLOG as distinct
from others such as expository, prophetic, procedural, etc. Each example is an entry in the Greater Lexicon and is labeled by its monolog subtype.
§ The use of the preposition is conditioned by position in the clause root and/or by the specific verb root within the predicate.

Display 1.10 Grammatical Formulas for REPORT MONOLOG (BN) Developed down to SENTENCE: Formulas 4-12

(4) REPORT MONOLOG (BN) =

Class: S(E)R(IA)L SEC(TION)
Slot: Nucleus (of REPORT MONOLOG)
Role: Interac(tion)
Cohesion: (1) Obligatory in occurrence, (2) (Lit Str of IE) With literary
    structural sequence of interaction and evaluation
GC 1; G1–11 *On May 26, 1940, as Hitler's . . . lives were saved.*

(5) SRL SEC =

Class: PROBLEM PARAGRAPH CLUSTER
Slot: Margin (of SRL SEC)
Role: Problem
Cohesion: (1) Obligatory, (2) Governs topic for the discourse,
    (3) Governs contending cast members
GC1.1; G1–4 *On May 26, . . . into the English Channel.*

(6) PROBLEM PARAGRAPH CLUSTER =

Class: TOPIC PARAGRAPH
Slot: Nucleus
Role: Problem
Cohesion: (1) Obligatory
GC1.1.1; G1–2 *On May 26, . . . into the English Channel.*

(7) SEQ PARAGRAPH CLUSTER =

Class: TOPIC PARAGRAPH
Slot: Nucleus
Role: Solution
Cohesion: (1) Obligatory, (2) With location of and activity of the
    principal cast members.
GC1.2.1; G5–9 *Then . . . May 27 . . . trying to fight them off.*

**Class: P(OIN)T OF REF(ERENCE)-C(O)NTR(A)ST PARAGRAPH
CL(U)ST(E)R**

Slot: Margin (of REPORT MONOLOG)
Role: Evaluation
Cohesion: (1) Optional in occurrence, (2) With Lit Str of IE
GC2; G12–13 *On June 18, Winston Churchill . . . For men . . . hour of
    greatest honor . . . Dunkirk.*

Class: SEQ(UENCE) PARAGRAPH CLUSTER

Slot: Nucleus (of SRL SEC)
Role: Solution
Cohesion: (1) Obligatory, (2) Topic governed by GC1.1, (3) Cast
    members governed by GC1.1
GC1.2; G5–11 *Then in the early hours . . . lives were saved.*

Class: CAUSE-EFFECT PARAGRAPH

Slot: Margin
Role: Amplification
Cohesion: ?
GC1.1.2; G3–4 *The mighty British navy . . . had been wiped out.*

Class: CAUSE-EFFECT PARAGRAPH

Slot: Margin
Role: Outcome
Cohesion: ?
GC1.2.2; G10–11 *Under that hell . . . lives were saved.*

(8) POINT OF REFERENCE-CONTRAST PARAGRAPH CLUSTER =

Class: (TOPIC PARAGRAPH) IND(EPENDENT) SENT(ENCE)
Slot: Margin
Role: Point of Reference
Cohesion: Obligatory
GC2.1; G12 *On June 18 . . . finest hour.*

Class: (TOPIC PARAGRAPH) IND SENT
Slot: Nucleus
Role: Contrast
Cohesion: Obligatory
GC2.2; G13 *For the men . . . at Dunkirk*

(9) TOPIC PARAGRAPH =

Class: INDEPENDENT SENTENCE (GC1.1.1; G1.
GC1.2.1.2.2.1; G8. GC2.1; G12. GC2.2; G13
SEQ SENT GC1.2.1.1; G5
Slot: Nucleus
Role: Topic
Cohesion: (1) Obligatory
G1 *On May 26 . . . retreated . . . port of Dunkirk.*
G5 *Then . . . miracle . . . unfold.*
G8 *As the morning sun . . . pulled onto the shore.*

Class: INDEPENDENT SENTENCE GC1.2.1.2.2.2; G9
Slot: Margin
Role: Circumstance
Cohesion: Optional
G9 *The cheers . . . were drowned . . . them off.*

Class: INDEPENDENT SENTENCE GC1.1.1.2; G2 MEANS-
ACCOMPLISHMENT SENTENCE CLUSTER
GC1.2.1.2; G6-9
Slot: Margin
Role: Amplification
Cohesion: Optional
G2 *From Dunkirk . . . English Channel,*
G6-9 *From everywhere . . . trying to fight them off.*

(10) CAUSE-EFFECT PARAGRAPH =

Class: IND SENT GC1.1.2.1. GC1.2.2.1
Slot: Nucleus
Role: Cause
Cohesion: Obligatory:
G3 *The mighty . . . evacuate the men.*
G10 *Under . . . days and nights.*

Class: EFFECT SENT GC1.1.2.2
(IND SENT) PAS(SIVE) T(RANSITIVE) CL(AUSE)
R(OO)T GC1.2.2.2
Slot: Margin
Role: Effect
Cohesion: Obligatory
G4 *Thus the Free World . . . wiped out.*
G11 *All together . . . were saved.*

Display 1.10 (*cont.*)

(11) MEANS-ACCOMPLISHMENT SENTENCE CLUSTER =

Class: GENERIC-SPECIFIC SENTENCE CLUSTER
Slot: Margin
Role: Means
Cohesion: ?
GC1.2.1.2.1; G6–7 *From everywhere . . . came . . . mine infested waters.*

Class: TOPIC PARAGRAPH
Slot: Nucleus
Role: Accomplishment
Cohesion: Obligatory
GC1.2.1.2.2; G8–9 *As the morning sunlight lighted . . . cheers . . . drowned out . . . fight them off.*

(12) GENERIC-SPECIFIC SENTENCE CLUSTER =

Class: INDEPENDENT SENTENCE
Slot: Margin
Role: General Means
Cohesion: ?
GC1.2.1.2.1.1; G6 *From everywhere . . . they came—poor fishermen . . . launches.*

Class: INDEPENDENT SENTENCE
Slot: Nucleus
Role: Specific Means
Cohesion: Obligatory
GC1.2.1.2.1.2; G7 *The first . . . set sail . . . across . . . water.*

Display 1.11 Grammatical Formulas for Sentence 1: Formulas 13-17

(13) INDEPENDENT SENTENCE =

Class: LOCATION PHRASE
Slot: Margin
Role: Time
Cohesion: ?
GC1.1.1.1.1 *On May 26, 1940*

Class: INDEPENDENT DECLARATIVE CLAUSE
Slot: Nucleus
Role: Proposition
Cohesion: (1) Obligatory, (2) With introducing a grammatically first or second ranked cast member. (Subject within an independent clause)
GC1.1.1.1.3 *British and French troops retreated . . . port of Dunkirk.*

Class: SIMULTANEOUS CLAUSE
Slot: Margin
Role: Simultaneous Action
Cohesion: (1) Optional, but probably context conditioned, (2) With introducing a grammatically third ranked cast member. (Subject within a dependent clause)
GC1.1.1.1.2 *as Hitler's . . . France*

(14) INDEPENDENT DECLARATIVE CLAUSE =

Class: BI-INTRANSITIVE CLAUSE ROOT
Slot: Nucleus
Role: Proposition
Cohesion: (1) Obligatory, (2) Choice of transitivity type is governed by focus of total discourse
GC1.1.1.1.3.1 *British and French troops retreated into the little French port of Dunkirk.*

Class: AGENT PHRASE
Slot: Margin
Role: Manner
Cohesion: (1) Optional, (2) Agrees with plural actor
GC1.1.1.1.3.2 *by the tens of thousands*

Display 1.11 (cont.)

(15) BI-INTRANSITIVE CLAUSE ROOT =

Class: NOUN PHRASE
Slot: Subject
Role: Actor
Cohesion: (1) Obligatory, (2) Governs number within the predicate.
GC1.1.1.1.2.2.1 *Hitler's armies*
GC1.1.1.1.3.1.1 *British and French troops*

Class: PLACE NOUN
LOCATION PHRASE
Slot: Adjunct
Role: Scope
Cohesion: Obligatory with *overrun*, optional with *retreat*
GC1.1.1.1.2.2.3 *France*
GC1.1.1.1.3.1.3 *into . . . Dunkirk.*

Class: (VERB PHRASE) VERB
Slot: Predicate
Role: Statement
Cohesion: (1) Obligatory, (2) Mutual requirement of a bi-intransitive verb root within the predicate with Subject-Actor and potential of Adjunct-Scope in the clause root, (3) Number governed by number of subject.
GC1.1.1.1.2.2.2 *overran*
GC1.1.1.1.3.1.2 *retreated*

(16) LOCATION PHRASE =

Class: LOCATION PREPOSITION
Slot: Margin
Role: Location
Cohesion: Obligatory
GC1.1.1.1.1.1 *on*
GC1.1.1.1.3.1.3.1 *into*

Class: INNER DATE PHRASE
NOUN PHRASE
Slot: Nucleus
Role: Location
Cohesion: (1) Obligatory, (2) Past time governed by REPORTED MONOLOG
GC1.1.1.1.1.2 *May 26, 1940*
GC1.1.1.1.3.1.3.2 *the little French port of Dunkirk*

(17) NOUN PHRASE =

Class: POSSESSED NOUN
    ARTICLE
Slot: Margin
Role: Specificity
Cohesion: (1) Obligatory if filler of nucleus is singular and Margin-
Specific Quantity does not also occur, otherwise is optional,
(2) Agrees in number with nucleus.
    GC1.1.1.2.2.1.1 *Hitler's*
    GC1.1.1.1.3.1.3.2.1 *the*

Class: NOUN
    NUMBER PHRASE
    NUCLEAR NOUN PHRASE
Slot: Nucleus
Role: Item
Cohesion: (1) Obligatory, (2) Governs number in Margins of Specificity
and of Specific Quantity, (3) If singular requires the presence of
either Margin of Specificity or of Specific Quantity, (4) Governs
number and gender of a pronoun used as referent.
    GC1.1.1.2.2.1.2 *armies*
    GC1.1.1.1.3.1.1.2 *troops*
    GC1.1.1.1.3.2.2.2 *tens of thousands*
    GC1.1.1.1.3.1.3.2.4 *port of Dunkirk*

Class: ADJECTIVE COORDINATE COMPLEX
    ADJECTIVE
    DERIVED ADJECTIVE
Slot: Margin
Role: Quality
Cohesion: (1) Optional, (2) Repeatable
    GC1.1.1.1.3.1.1.1 *British and French troops*
    GC1.1.1.3.1.3.2.2 *little*
    GC1.1.1.1.3.1.3.2.3 *French*

Transitivity cohesion gives the contrastive features of major types of clause roots (nuclear element of the clause). It correlates the number and kinds (role differences) of terms (free forms) which may be tolerated by a given class of verb roots. If a term may occur with virtually any verb root, it is considered to be a clause margin rather than a clause nuclear element. The nuclear elements, other than the predicate, are participant tagmemes. For a fuller statement of transitivity, please see Pike and Pike (1982). Although the transitivity cohesion is a mutual agreement feature of all the participant tagmemes with the predicate, by convention we mark it only in the predicate. The encoding clause root correlates the encoding verb root class: *say, report, affirm, ask, think* . . . with the Subject-Actor (in the encoding clause root actor is etic speaker), Adjunct-Undergoer (etic quotation), and Adjunct-Scope (etic hearer). The decoding clause root correlates the decoding verb root class: *hear, understand,* . . . with Subject-Actor (etic hearer), Adjunct-Undergoer (etic quotation), and Adjunct-Scope (etic speaker). These two clause roots are a subset of bitransitive clause roots in that actor, undergoer, and scope occur; in this instance the scope is optional when not in the axis underlying a whole discourse. Those clause roots which in their full, active declarative form occur with actor and undergoer are transitive; those with actor and scope are bi-transitive; those with only actor are intransitive; those with item and complement (not a participant tagmeme) are equative; and those with item, complement, and scope are bi-equative.

Much work remains to be done with the cohesion features, especially of intermediate levels of structure. We merely mention some of the more interesting ones: (1) In Formula 4 REPORT MONOLOG the two constituents govern the grammatical structure of the whole discourse in such a way that it must be appropriate for the roles of interaction and evaluation. (2) In Formula 5 SRL SEC the first immediate constituent with the role of problem governs the topic for the discourse as well as the list of the contending cast members. (3) In Formula 13 INDEPENDENT SENTENCE we see the cohesion which is relevant to the grammatical ranking of the members of the cast—according to the relative grammatical prominence in which each is introduced. The two highest ranks are introduced as subject within the INDEPENDENT DECLARATIVE CLAUSE, the third constituent of the Formula 13. Normal prominence of that subject is used to introduce the second rank: *British and French troops* G1.3, *The mighty British navy* G3, *the Free World* G4.1, *and Winston Churchill* G12.2. However, extra prominence of that subject is used to introduce BATHTUB NAVY thus giving it first rank. This is achieved by the off-norm use of the pronoun *they* with its references following, in G6 *From everywhere . . . they came—poor fishermen with creaky, beat-up fishing boats, . . . motor launches*. There is only one third ranked cast member: *Hitler's armies* G1.2. It is introduced as subject within the dependent clause of the second constituent of Formula 13: SIMULTANEOUS CLAUSE. We do not present our analysis of the lower level constructions which introduce fourth ranked members: *the Luftwaffe* G9.1 and *British Spitfires* G9.3, but they are found as coordinates within the adjunct-actor of a passive clause root. (4) The last grammatical feature that we mention here is especially important to the whole discourse: the choice of which type of clause root is chosen for the nucleus of a clause—whether active or passive, or which transitivity type. This is governed by which element of the clause root must be in focus.

This concludes the highlights of our grammatical analysis. More details are to be found in the displays. However, to be able to produce utterances which would approach grammatical acceptability, each construction needs a formula; then each morpheme class needs to be listed. For such a tight description see Pike and Pike (1982), Display 1.1 and Appendix 2.

1.3 THE REFERENTIAL STRUCTURE OF BN, THE BATTLE OF DUNKIRK

1.3.1 General characteristics of referential structure

The referential structure of a stream of speech is by far the largest and most complex of the three hierarchies. As mentioned above, it concerns that to which speech refers, the *communication referents*. The etic structure of the system approaches the extent of human perception—that which people talk about. Even as a phonetic system reflects the sum total of all contrastive speech sounds of known languages of the world, so the etic system of reference reflects all the identifiable cultural factors in cultures of the world. The speech of any one language-cultural group affords the linguist a prime source for discovering the emic referential system of that group.

1.3.1.1 *The referential tagmeme*

Each unit in this structure represents a tagmeme exhibiting the four contrastive-identificational features discussed in grammar: class, slot, role, and cohesion.

Referential **class** is the substance of reference: the events, identities, attribute relations, and place relations. These answer the question of what is going on and who or what is involved in those happenings. **Slot** answers the question of where those happenings are going on—where in time and space, within what immediately larger context of happenings, and with what prominence in relation to other immediate constituents of that larger structure. **Role** answers the question of what purpose or reason do those involved in the events have for those actions which take place. **Cohesion** asks what system controls or limits the kinds of substance (events, etc.) which actually occur. These have to do with (1) the world view of the members of the cast, (2) reality or irreality, (3) success or failure, (4) notions of appropriateness in government or personal behavior, (5) personality constraints, etc.

1.3.1.2 *Some differences between grammar and reference*

Sequence. Grammatical sequence is the order in which things are told. Referential sequence is the chronological sequence or the order in which things happen, or the logical order of cause and effect, etc. Referential sequence admits simultaneity whereas grammar does not; many things may happen at once, but because words are spoken one at a time, two things can't be said at once (excepting, for example, in puns). Also chronological order is fixed, whereas the grammatical order is seldom fixed. One has to enter a store before he can make a purchase in that store, but in English he can talk about the purchase before he need talk about entering the store: *I made a purchase after I entered the store*. The word *after* informs the hearer of the actual chronological sequence.

Paraphrase Set. Another difference between reference and grammar is that events, identities, etc. can be expressed in a variety of grammatical forms. Examples of two particular events: *The dogs barked. The baby woke up*. We can talk about the same two events without repeating more than the morpheme *the* in: *Because Fido and Buster yapped at each other, the little one's sleep was interrupted*. Other ways of talking about the same events might be: *The barking dogs woke up the baby,* or *The baby was awakened by the noise of the dogs*. We accept those as a paraphrase set only if the speaker affirms that that is what he was saying, implying that any differences are not crucial to his interests. We say that the sameness of a paraphrase set is essentially referential and the differences are essentially grammatical. Each different paraphrase above is talking about more than one dog making noise and a baby waking up. One paraphrase gives the information that there were two dogs; several state specifically that the barking of the dogs was responsible for waking up the baby. That lets us know, incidentally, that even though the first two sentences *The dogs barked. The baby woke up.* are not marked for either cause or effect, none the less they have those grammatical roles respectively.

If part of the purpose of the speaker were to identify the dogs by name, then the alternate statements would not be accepted as paraphrases. The purpose of the speaker is crucial.

Focus or Prominence. There is a difference in focus in the various members of the paraphrase set mentioned above, such as active versus passive constructions. These we consider as grammatical focus. Referential focus is achieved by specific happenings such as shouting, pointing, entering a room at a moment when the attention of everyone may be captured, wearing outstanding clothing, or behaving in a way different from the people around, so that they are aware of it, etc.

1.3.2 Referential event classes and their roles in BN

In studying phonological structure we use phonetic charts to place before us all the phonological elements which we deem relevant for our immediate analysis. We use grammatical workcharts to do the same for grammar. In order to have before us the elements necessary for a referential analysis of a text we list in chronological order the smallest events that we understand to have happened as communicated to us by the stream of speech. BN is referentially HISTORICAL MACRO EVENT specifically The Battle of Dunkirk. Hence the events in Display 1.12 are those events of the battle which we understand from BN. Opposite each event we state its role—the purpose or reason for the occurrence of that event. Purpose takes precedence over reason and is introduced by *to*, whereas reason is introduced by *because*. The purposes or reasons which are not stated in the text, but which we have deduced, are placed in square brackets. To the extent that we have misjudged either the role or an event, to that extent we have misunderstood the stream of speech. State is considered to be derivative of action, hence is stated as action. The numbers of the events reflect essentially chronological order; letters with any one number suggest simultaneity of occurrence. Those numbers are prefaced by RE (Referential Event) and are used for cross reference in the displays as well as in discussion of our analysis. The time line is a simple one, labelled by the times stated in the text. In as much as events are placed on the time line, we phrase the event

Display 1.12 List of Referential Substance (Class) and Role of Events of the HISTORICAL MACRO EVENT, The Battle of Dunkirk (BN)

Time:	Referential Class of Events*	Referential Role (Purpose or Reason of Event in First Column)†
Before May 26, 1940	(RE1)‡ THE BRITISH EMPIRE AND COMMONWEALTH FUNCTION. G12.4	[Because of many historical incidents.]§
	(RE2a) GERMAN MILITARY MAINTAINS U-BOATS IN ENGLISH CHANNEL. G7.4	[To diminish allied shipping.]
	(b) GERMAN MILITARY LAYS MINES IN ENGLISH CHANNEL. G7.4	[To diminish allied shipping.]
	(RE3) BRITISH NAVY CAN'T GO INTO DUNKIRK BEACHES AND EVACUATE MEN. G3.1	Because it has too few ships which are sufficiently small and agile.
	(RE4) HITLER'S ARMIES OVERRUN FRANCE. G1.2	[To rule France.]
May 26	(RE5a) TENS OF THOUSANDS OF BRITISH AND FRENCH TROOPS RETREAT INTO DUNKIRK. G1.3	[To avoid being wiped out by German military.]
	(b) GERMAN MILITARY TRAPS TROOPS G2, 9.1–2, 10.1	Because there is no way for troops to cross the English Channel.
	(RE6a) FREE WORLD SITS BY RADIO. G4.1	[To hear news of troops.]
	(b) FREE WORLD HEARS REPORTS OF DUNKIRK ACTIVITIES. G4.1	[Because of broadcasting system.]
	(c) FREE WORLD FEARS THAT THE VAST ARMIES OF BRAVE MEN WILL BE WIPED OUT. G4.2	Because men are trapped.
	(d) FREE WORLD BECOMES FRUSTRATED. G4.1	Because Free World can do nothing to help.
Early hours of May 27	(e) FREE WORLD BECOMES EXTREMELY DISTRESSED G4.1	[Because they fear that the armies will be wiped out.]

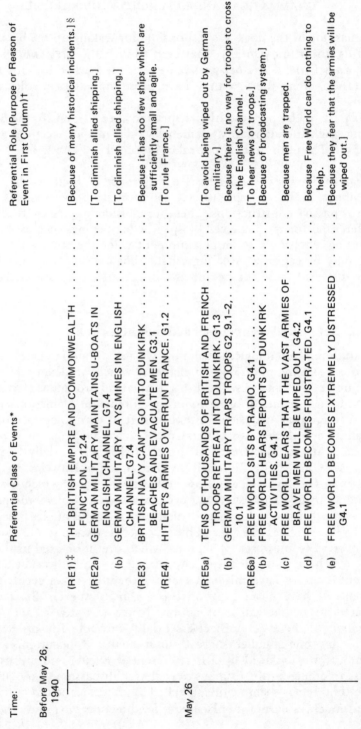

(RE7a)	A MIRACLE BEGINS. G5.3 · · · · · · · · ·	[Because unexpected people risk their lives to provide escape for trapped troops.]
(b)	POOR F(ISHERMEN), N(OBLEMEN), S(PORTSMEN) CAN'T DEFEND THEMSELVES. G7.2 · · · ·	Because they don't have guns.
(c)	F, N, S WEAR THEIR OWN CLOTHING. G7.2 · · · ·	Because they don't have uniforms.
(d)	F, N, S COME FROM ALL PARTS OF BRITISH ISLES TO SHEERNESS WITH THEIR SMALL BOATS. G7.2 · · · ·	[To try to rescue trapped troops.]
(RE8)	F, N, S CAPTAIN THEIR OWN BOATS. G7.2 · · · ·	[Because they are the ones available to them.]
(RE9)	MOTLEY FLEET SETS SAIL FROM SHEERNESS G7.3 · · · ·	[Because it is a designated place to start crossing the English Channel.]
(RE10)	MOTLEY FLEET PUTT-PUTTS ACROSS ENGLISH CHANNEL. G7.4 · · · ·	[To get to Dunkirk.]
(RE11a)	LUFTWAFFE FLIES OVER DUNKIRK. G9.1 · · · ·	[To destroy the allied forces.]
(b)	LUFTWAFFE ROARS. G9.1 · · · ·	[Because Luftwaffe engines are powerful (and because of ammunition explosions).]
(c)	LUFTWAFFE STRAFES AND BOMBS BEACHES. G9.2 · · · ·	[To destroy the allied forces.]
(d)	BRITISH SPITFIRES TRY TO FIGHT OFF LUFTWAFFE WITH THEIR GUNS. G9.3 · · · ·	[To prevent Luftwaffe from destroying trapped troops.]
(e)	SPITFIRE GUNS CRACKLE. G9.3 · · · ·	[Because the guns are being used to shoot Luftwaffe.]
(RE12a)	FIRST OF HUNDREDS OF SMALL BOATS PULL ONTO DUNKIRK SHORE. G8.2 · · · ·	[To rescue troops and because they have escaped hazards of the Channel.]
(b)	SOLDIERS CHEER. G9.1 · · · ·	[Because they have hope of surviving.]
(c)	AERIAL COMBAT DROWNS OUT CHEERS. G9 · · · ·	[Because the combat is very loud.]
(d)	SOLDIERS GET IN BOATS. G10.2, 11 · · · ·	[To escape.]
(RE13)	SMALL BOATS ARRIVE AT A SAFE PLACE. G11 · · · ·	[Because they have escaped the Channel hazards.]
(RE14)	OFFICIALS COUNT TROOPS WHO REACH SAFETY. G11 · · · ·	[To account for personnel.]
(RE15)	GERMAN MILITARY DOES NOT WIPE OUT VAST ARMIES. G5.3, 10, 11, 12.6, 13 · · · ·	[Because Bathtub Navy, Spitfires, and others have worked valiantly.]

Events repeated with etic varieties

nine days and nights

By moonlight

Sun-up
May 27

Display 1.12 (cont.)

June 5

(RE16) OFFICIALS REPORT THE SAVING OF 338,226 BRITISH AND FRENCH TROOPS. G11 . . . . [To let people (including Free World) know what has been accomplished.]

(RE17) BN JUDGES WORK ON DUNKIRK BEACHES AS THEIR FINEST WORK. G13 . . . . [Because it was focus of danger and had to do directly with troops.]

(RE18) CHURCHILL EXPECTS FUTURE GENERATIONS, 1000 YEARS HENCE, TO JUDGE THE DUNKIRK MIRACLE TO BE BRITAIN'S FINEST HOUR. G12.4-5 . . . . [Because Britishers have done a courageous and honorable job.]

June 18

(RE19) CHURCHILL CHALLENGES BRITISHERS TO DO THEIR DUTY COURAGEOUSLY AND HONORABLY. G12 . . . . . . [Because he is pleased with what they have done, but must do a great deal more.]

(RE20) CHURCHILL TELLS OF HIS EXPECTATION OF FUTURE GENERATIONS. G12.4-6 . . . . . . [To encourage Britishers.]

(RE21a) SHERMAN SELECTS DUNKIRK ACTIVITIES AS BEING EXCEPTIONALLY COURAGEOUS AND HONORABLE. G Total article . . . . . . [Because he is looking for incidents to encourage people (readers of *Reader's Digest*).]

(b) SHERMAN JUDGES THAT IN THE MINDS OF MEN IN HIS MAJESTY'S BATHTUB NAVY THE FINEST HOUR WAS THEIR TIME ON DUNKIRK BEACHES. G13 . . . . . . [Because he recognizes that it was there that occurred the peak of courageous and honorable action of the F, N, S.]

(c) SHERMAN SELECTS THE CHURCHILL STATEMENT . . . . . . [To present context in which Sherman's judgement is validated.]

May 1971

(RE22) SHERMAN TELLS (WRITES) 'THE BATHTUB NAVY' FROM HIS PERSPECTIVE. . . . . . . [To tell others (including authors) what he thinks is important relative to the miracle of Dunkirk.]

(RE23) AUTHORS HEAR (READ) 'THE BATHTUB NAVY'. . . . . . . To receive pleasure and information.

(RE24a) AUTHORS MAKE A GRAMMATICAL ANALYSIS . . . . To analyze their understanding of BN
OF BN. through grammatical structure.
(b) AUTHORS MAKE A REFERENTIAL ANALYSIS . . . . To analyze their understanding of BN
OF BN. through referential structure.

(RE25) PEOPLE JUDGE BRITISH EMPIRE'S FINEST HOUR . . . . [Because everyone remembers it as being
TO BE THE DUNKIRK MIRACLE. G12 very courageous and honorable and
contributing toward the survival of the
British Empire.]

2940
(a very
long time in future)

* This is a list of the smallest events relevant to the understanding of the text. Relevancy is judged by the authors who are presumably a typical sample of Sherman's audience. The authors try to state these in terms of the actors and their action; states are considered to be derivative of an action. Times involved are accounted for in the time lines; props, space, attributes, etc. are included in the statement of these events. For simplicity the authors have substituted the actions of writing, publishing, and reading (actions in parentheses) with telling and hearing.

† These roles answer the question of *Why?* (purpose or reason); hence are of two types: (1) The event is intended to be a cause affecting something else and is introduced by *To*, or (2) The event is the result (effect) of some prior cause or condition and is introduced by *Because*. Purpose takes precedence over reason.

‡ The numbers indicate essentially the chronological order of events. Those numbers with arrows pointing to a time line are those events which more conspicuously occur over the span of time indicated by the line. Letters under any one number suggest simultaneity of occurrence. A broken line indicates future time.

§ Square brackets enclose the purpose/reason which the authors have deduced; if their deduction is wrong, to that extent they have misunderstood Sherman, or history.

as of the **now** time relative to its place on that line. The text source of each event is labelled by its G (Grammatical Sentence) number.

This list needs to be detailed only to the extent that allows the hearer to understand what the speaker intends, and allows the hearer to tell a comparable narrative. This is analogous to the phonetic detail necessary for the hearer to distinguish contrastive sounds of a language and to be able to speak using those contrasts—albeit with an 'accent.'

Note that RE 1 THE BRITISH EMPIRE AND COMMON-WEALTH FUNCTION derives from G12.4 *if the British Empire and its Commonwealth last . . .*; the arrow from that event reaches to the time line extending from 'Before May 26, 1940' to '2940 A.D. (a very long time).' Also, note that RE2a GERMAN MILITARY MAIN-TAINS U-BOATS IN ENGLISH CHANNEL derives from G7.4 . . . *U-boat . . . infested water*. Thus we see that referential events are not co-extensive with grammatical propositions. None the less they exhibit an independence in the referential hierarchy comparable to that which the clause and sentence do in the grammatical hierarchy, in contrast to the relative dependency of their respective lower levels.

From our first etic list, some events had to be added in order to understand the text, while others could be omitted as going into detail unnecessary to the understanding of this particular text. Also a first guess as to role was doubtful enough for several to be listed for a single event, but was then revised as the emic structure of the text became more apparent. Some of these tentatively assigned roles were eliminated; others were seen to be relevant to a sequence of events rather than to a single one; while other events such as RE6a were judged to have more than one role.

Another factor is often present: an event may have an incidental role versus a crucial role. This would be true if a parent asked a child to go to the store to buy a loaf of bread, both because the bread might be required for a meal, but more essentially because the parent wanted to prepare a surprise for the child in his absence. We did not find such dual roles for an event in this text (but possibly there is such for the identity constituent *a thousand years* which will be discussed below). Another kind of role differentiation is possible, but not one which is found in this text: a person may make an identical statement at different times and yet the two events may have different roles. Consider, for example, the child who tells his mother, *'I'm thirsty. I need a drink.'* on coming into the house 'in order to quench his thirst' versus when he says the same thing while being put to bed, not in order to quench his thirst, but rather 'in order to delay being put to bed.' Although the grammatical statement is the same, the two events are different, partly because the purpose or role is different.

Returning to the present text, we recognize that etically there are many more roles for events than we have listed. Consider RE5a 'Tens of thousands of . . . troops retreat . . .' to which we have attributed the role of 'in order to avoid being wiped out . . .,' but no doubt some troops retreated under military orders and had no choice other than to follow those orders. Perhaps both roles should be included; however, we believe that 'to avoid being wiped out . . .' is likely to be the reason that many of those troops would have agreed to. In addition we judge that that is all the detail of purpose that is necessary for us to understand what Sherman was trying to tell us. If we are mistaken in that, then we have misunderstood some of what Sherman was saying.

In discussing with an English friend the role of RE9 'Motley fleet sets sail from Sheerness' which is 'Because it is a designated place to start crossing the English Channel,' he questioned our understanding, saying that it was only the first of the fleet to start out from there; other parts of that fleet started from other unspecified seaports. We concur in his judgement; we were probably wrong.

Included in our list of events are negative happenings. The first is RE3; G3.1 that the navy can't go in to the Dunkirk beaches. This negative event is crucial in describing the problem. Another negative event is that the German forces don't wipe out the trapped troops —another significant non-happening. Thus, we see that relevant events that don't occur must be included in order to understand what is being said.

1.3.3 Segmentation of the referential structure into vectors and complexes down to events

There are five groups of the cast acting in the HISTORICAL MACRO EVENT, the Battle of Dunkirk. Each of them is involved in a sequence of purposeful events: (1) the German military, (2) the Free World, (3) the Allied personnel, (4) the current evaluators, and (5) the projected evaluators. Each of these groups pursues its line of activities, each for its own distinct purposes. These separate, purposeful sequences of events form the five major referential sections or vectors of this text; see Display 1.13A. In Displays 1.13A, 1.13B, and 1.13C the vectors are developed down to the individual events which are listed in Display 1.12. The three triangles with solid lines, each under a complex (CX), indicate the only units not developed down to event. The two triangles with broken lines are developed down to event in the formulas, but not in the tree diagrams. In Displays 1.13A, 1.13B, 1.13C, 1.15, and 1.17, in the interest of simplicity, we have entered only the class. This is in order to show more clearly the related groups we have posited in relation to the various levels of the hierarchy. We group together those events which are tied together by the common overall purpose of a given member or group of the cast. Each event is more closely tied to another of the group than it is related to any other event or groups of events.

There are four constituents in GERMAN ATTACK VECTOR RC1 to be seen in Display 1.13A and in Display 1.14, Formula 19; the last constituent is GERMAN MILITARY DOESN'T WIPE OUT VAST ARMIES RC1.4. This last constituent (event) also occurs in MIRACLE COMPLEX (CX) as RC3.3.4, Display 1.13B and Display 1.14, Formula 25. In MIRACLE COMPLEX it is an event coherent with success (of allied forces) whereas in the former construction it is an event coherent with failure (of German forces). RE5b GERMAN MILITARY TRAPS TROOPS has just the reverse cohesion. Within the GERMAN ATTACK VECTOR, as RC1.2.2, Formula 21, it is an event coherent with success, but as RC3.2.3, Formula 24, within the DILEMMA CX it is an event coherent with failure (of the allied forces). RE11, having to do with the fighting between the Luftwaffe and the Spitfires, is part of two different vectors: German versus the allied related vector within RC1.3, Display 1.13A, and RC3.3.3.2, Display 1.13C, respectively.

Such a difference in cohesion depending on the point of view of different cast members is very apparent in accusations of one party against another. In an incident reported in a narrative in Isirawa of Irian Jaya, a neighbor was accused of witchcraft which he denied. The event was real for the accusers, nonexistent for the accused, and up to the time we were studying the text the government had not yet ruled as to whether the event was coherent with reality or non-reality; the man was still being held for trial (Erickson and Evelyn G. Pike, 1976: 63-93).

There are at least two tagmemes which are repeated: RC3.3.3 ACCOMPLISHMENT CX and RC3.3.5.1 OFFICIALS COUNT TROOPS WHO REACH SAFETY; see Displays 1.13B and C. These are repeated over the nine days and nights for an unknown number of times. The actual happenings of each repetition were certainly different, but we judge the differences to be only etic differences involving the same or substitutable personnel and equipment, acting essentially emically at this level of analysis—in the 'same' way to accomplish the same purposes.

HISTORICAL MACRO EVENT
The Battle of Dunkirk (BN)
RC0.2.2.2; RE24b

RC1
GERMAN ATTACK VECTOR
RE2, 4, 5b, 11, 12c, 15; G1.2, 2, 4.2, 7.4, 9

RC2
FREE WORLD (FW) DESPAIR
VECTOR RE6; G4

RC3
RESCUE VECTOR
RE1, 3, 5a-b, 7-16; G12.4, 1-11

RC4
EVALUATION VECTOR
RE17-20; G12-13

RC5
PEOPLE JUDGE BRITISH
EMPIRE'S FINEST HOUR
TO BE THE DUNKIRK
MIRACLE RE25; G12

RC1.1
SEA COMPLEX
(CX)
RE2a-b;
G7.4

RC1.2
LAND
CX
RE4-5;
G1.2, 2, 4.2

RC1.3
AIR CX
RE11a-c; 12c
G9.1-2, 10.1

RC1.4
GERMAN MILITARY
DOESN'T WIPE OUT
VAST ARMIES
RE15; G5.3, 10-11,
12.6, 13

RC2.1
FW SITS BY RADIO.
RE6a; G4.1

RC2.2
FW HEARS
REPORTS OF
DUNKIRK
ACTIVITIES.
RE6b; G4.1

RC2.3
FW FEARS
THAT THE VAST
ARMIES OF BRAVE
MEN WILL BE
WIPED OUT.
RE6c; G4.2

RC2.4
FW BECOMES
FRUSTRATED
RE6d, G4.1

RC2.5
FW BECOMES
EXTREMELY
DISTRESSED.
RE6e; G4.1

RC4.1
BN JUDGES WORK ON DK
BEACHES AS THEIR FINEST
WORK. RE17; G13

RC4.2
CHURCHILL CX
RE 18-20; G12

Display 1.13B Referential Tree Diagram of the HISTORICAL MACRO EVENT, The Battle of Dunkirk (BN); Developed Down to Event: Classes Only (Continued)

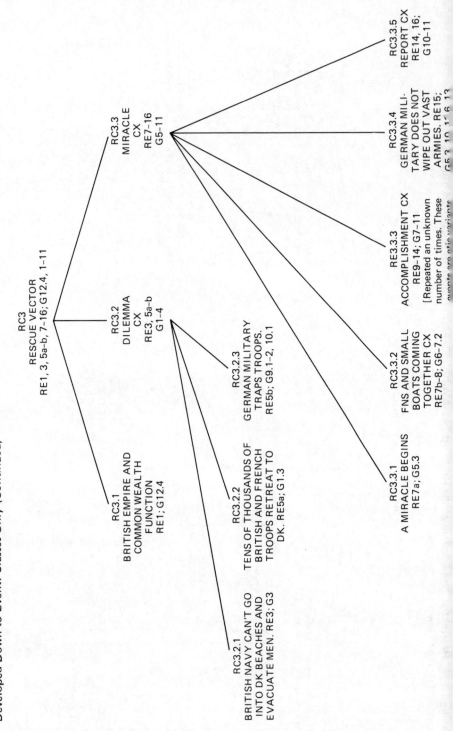

RC4.2
CHURCHILL CX
RE18–20; G12

RC4.2.1
CHURCHILL EXPECTS
FUTURE GENERATIONS
1,000 YEARS HENCE TO JUDGE
THE DK MIRACLE TO BE
BRITAIN'S FINEST HOUR.
RE18; G12

RC4.2.2
CHURCHILL SPEECH CX
RE19–20; G12

RC4.2.2.1
CHURCHILL
CHALLENGES
B's TO DO
THEIR DUTY
COURAGEOUSLY
AND HONORABLY.
RE19; G12

RC4.2.2.2
CHURCHILL
TELLS OF HIS
EXPECTATIONS
OF FUTURE
GENERATIONS.
RE20; G12

RE3.3.5.2
OFFICIALS REPORT
THE SAVING OF
338,266 BRITISH
AND FRENCH
TROOPS RE16; G11

RC3.3.5
REPORT CX
RE14, 16;
G10–11

RC3.3.5.1
OFFICIALS COUNT
TROOPS WHO REACH
SAFETY. RE14; G11

RC3.3.3.4
SMALL BOATS ARRIVE AT A SAFE
PLACE. RE13; G11

RC3.3.3.3.3.4
SOLDIERS GET IN
BOATS. RE12d;
G10.2–11

RC3.3.3
ACCOMPLISHMENT CX
RE9–14; G7–11
[Repeated an unknown
number of times. These
events are etic variants
of those mentioned in
the text.]

RC3.3.3.3
ARRIVAL CX
RE12; G8.2–G11

RC3.3.3.3.3
AERIAL COMBAT DROWNS
OUT CHEERS.
RE12c; G9

RC3.3.3.3.2
SOLDIERS CHEER.
RE12b; G9.1

RC3.3.3.2
BEACH CX
RE11; G9

RC3.3.3.3.3.1
FIRST OF HUNDREDS OF
SMALL BOATS PULL ON
DK SHORE.
RE12a; G8.2

RC3.3.3.1
CHANNEL CROSSING
CX RE9–10, G7.3–4

1.3.4 Referential slot, role, and cohesion of events as seen in formulas

The classes in the tree displays are for the most part simply the substance found in this one text—very particular classes. Actually we suggest the general referential class for the whole text to be HISTORICAL MACRO EVENT of which the Battle of Dunkirk is a specific instance. In the lower levels of this text also we have several examples of a single more general referential class which will be discussed below. We would expect that with the study of many more texts we would find that more of the classes of this text are instances of a more general class. In the formulas we add to class the tagmeme features of slots, role, and cohesion.

For slot we include the relative prominence of the tagmeme in relation to other immediate constituents of the including structure. This, as for the grammar, is nucleus versus margin. In Formula 18 of Display 1.14 we have the first referential formula of the HISTORI-CAL MACRO EVENT; there are five immediate constituents, which we mentioned above. Of these the RESCUE VECTOR is the nucleus and the other four are margins. The two margins preceding the RESCUE VECTOR point toward confrontation and the events which that would entail in RESCUE VECTOR, whereas the post nuclear margins refer back to what in fact did happen in the confrontation. The RESCUE VECTOR is the largest constituent, presents the activity of the hero group of cast members (His Majesty's Bathtub Navy), and presents the peak of action and its results. The marginal constituents of that RESCUE VECTOR present the activities of the lesser cast members; the first has to do with the antagonist group in the GERMAN ATTACK VECTOR, the second with the onlooking group, then the post margins have to do with evaluators of the events in that RESCUE VECTOR. All these factors point to the nuclearity of the RESCUE VECTOR.

Nuclearity versus marginality is not always as clearly marked as in the structure just mentioned. Consider Formula 19 in Display 1.14, the GERMAN ATTACK VECTOR. The SEA COMPLEX is marginal in that the maintaining of U-boats and laying of mines is not involved in the focal point of the Battle of Dunkirk, whereas the LAND COM-PLEX and AIR COMPLEX are. We have judged both of these latter to be nuclear. However, since only the Luftwaffe could be at the actual central location of the battle, perhaps it alone should be considered to be the nucleus of that complex; in that case it would be well to treat the LAND COMPLEX as a primary margin and the SEA COMPLEX as a secondary margin. This problem points up the

Display 1.14 Referential Formulas for HISTORICAL MACRO EVENT, The Battle of Dunkirk (BN), Developed Down to Event: Formulas 18–31

(18) HISTORICAL MACRO EVENT =

Class: GERMAN ATTACK VECTOR
Slot: Margin; By May, June 1940; France, English Channel
Role: To dominate Europe
Cohesion: With failure
RC1; RE2, 4, 5b, 11, 12c, 15; G1.2, 2.7, 4, 9

Class: RESCUE VECTOR
Slot: Nucleus; Prior to May 26 through June 5; World of the Empire
Role: To save vast armies
Cohesion: With success
RC3; RE1, 3, 5a–b, 7–16, G12.4, 1–11

Class: PEOPLE JUDGE BRITISH EMPIRE'S FINEST HOUR TO BE
          THE DUNKIRK MIRACLE
Slot: Margin; Projected time to be 1000 years beyond June 18 (a long
          time in the future); in the world
Role: Because Dunkirk activities were a peak of courage
Cohesion: With the desired national image of the future
RC5; RE25; G12

Class: FREE WORLD DESPAIR VECTOR
Slot: Margin; May, June 1940; Free World
Role: Because of concern for European situation
Cohesion: With reality
RC2; RE6; G4

Class: EVALUATION VECTOR
Slot: Margin; June 1940; British Isles; English Channel; Dunkirk
Role: To evaluate activities in relation to goals
Cohesion: With human need to judge activities in relation to personal
          and national values.
RC4; RE17–20; G12–13

(19) GERMAN ATTACK VECTOR =

Class: SEA COMPLEX
Slot: Margin; before May 26; English Channel
Role: To diminish enemy shipping
Cohesion: With German national conquest plan
RC1.1; RE2a–b; G7.4

Class: AIR COMPLEX
Slot: Nucleus; May 26–June 5; Over and around Dunkirk
Role: To wipe out vast armies
Cohesion: With German national conquest plan
RC1.3; RE11a–c, 12c; G9.1–2, 10.1

Class: LAND COMPLEX
Slot: Nucleus; May 26; France
Role: To wipe out vast armies
Cohesion: With German national conquest plan
RC1.2; RE4–5; G1.2, 2, 4.2

Class: GERMAN MILITARY DOESN'T WIPE OUT VAST ARMIES
Slot: Nucleus; By June 5, 1940; Dunkirk area
Role: Because of allied concerted effort
Cohesion: With failure
RC1.4; RE15; G5.3, 10–11, 12.6, 13

Display 1.14 (cont.)

(20) SEA COMPLEX =

Class: GERMAN MILITARY MAINTAINS U-BOATS IN ENGLISH CHANNEL
Slot: Nucleus; Same date and place as RC1.1
Role: Same as for RC1.1
Cohesion: (1) Same as RC1.1, 2) Repeatable
RC1.1.1; RE2a; G7.4

Class: GERMAN MILITARY LAYS MINES IN ENGLISH CHANNEL
Slot: } Since this is a repetition of the preceding tagmeme,
Role: } only the class differs.
Cohesion:
RC1.1.2; RE2b; G7.4

(21) LAND COMPLEX =

Class: HITLER'S ARMIES OVERRUN FRANCE
Slot: Margin; Same date and place as RC1.2
Role: To rule France
Cohesion: With success
RC1.2.1; RE4; G1.2

Class: GERMAN MILITARY TRAPS TROOPS
Slot: Nucleus; Shortly before and up to May 26; Dunkirk area
Role: Because there is no way for troops to escape
Cohesion: With success
RC1.2.2; RE5b; G2, 9.1, 2, 10.1

(22) FREE WORLD DESPAIR VECTOR =

Class: FREE WORLD SITS BY RADIO
Slot: Margin; Same date and place as for RC2.
Role: To hear news
Cohesion: Same as for RC2.
RC2.1; RE6a; G4.1

Class: FREE WORLD HEARS REPORTS OF DUNKIRK ACTIVITIES
Slot: Nucleus; Same date and place as for RC2
Role: Because of broadcasting system
Cohesion: Same as for RC2
RC2.2; RE6b; G4.1

Class: FREE WORLD FEARS THAT THE VAST ARMIES OF BRAVE MEN WILL BE WIPED OUT
Slot: Margin; Same date and place as for RC2
Role: Because men are trapped
Cohesion: Same as for RC2
RC2.3; RE6c; G4.2

Class: FREE WORLD BECOMES FRUSTRATED
Slot: Margin; Same date and place as for RC2
Role: Because Free World can do nothing to help
Cohesion: Same as for RC2
RC2.4; RE6d; G4.1

Class: FREE WORLD BECOMES EXTREMELY DISTRESSED
Slot: Margin; Same date and place as for RC2
Role: Because they fear that the armies will be wiped out.
Cohesion: Same as for RC2
RC2.5; RE6e; G4.1

(23) RESCUE VECTOR =

Class: THE BRITISH EMPIRE AND COMMONWEALTH FUNCTION
Slot: Margin; Before May 26, 1940; British Isles, etc.
Role: Because of many historical incidents
Cohesion: With reality
RC3.1; RE1; G12.4

Class: MIRACLE COMPLEX
Slot: Nucleus; May 27–June 5; British Isles, English Channel, Dunkirk
Role: Because of total effort of allied forces
Cohesion: Same as for RC3
RC3.3; RE7–16; G5–11

Class: DILEMMA COMPLEX
Slot: Margin; Before May 26, 1940; Dunkirk
Role: Because of power of German military and weakness of allied forces
Cohesion: With reality
RC3.2; RE3, 5a, 5b; G1–4

(24) DILEMMA COMPLEX =

Class: BRITISH NAVY CAN'T GO INTO DUNKIRK BEACHES
Slot: Margin; Before May 26, 1940; Same place as for RC3.2
Role: Because it has too few ships which are sufficiently small and agile
Cohesion: With failure
RC3.2.1; RE3; G3

Class: GERMAN MILITARY TRAPS TROOPS
Slot: Nucleus; May 26; Same place as for RC3.2
Role: Because there is no way for the troops to cross the English Channel
Cohesion: With failure
RC3.2.3; RE5b; G9.1–2, 10.1

Class: TENS OF THOUSANDS OF BRITISH AND FRENCH TROOPS RETREAT TO DUNKIRK
Slot: Margin; May 26; Same place as for RC3.2
Role: To avoid being wiped out by German military
Cohesion: Same as for RC3.2
RC3.2.2; RE5a, G1.3

Display 1.14 (*cont.*)

(25) MIRACLE COMPLEX =

Class: A MIRACLE BEGINS
Slot: Margin; Early hours of May 27; British Isles
Role: Because people risk their lives to provide escape for trapped troops
Cohesion: Same as for RC3
RC3.3.1; RE7a; G5.3

Class: ACCOMPLISHMENT COMPLEX (Repeatable)
Slot: Nucleus; May 27–June 5; English Channel, Dunkirk
Role: Same as for RC3
Cohesion: Same as for RC3
RC3.3; RE9-14; G7-11
Note: This tagmeme is repeated an unknown number of times. Each repetition is an etic variant of the other.

Class: REPORT COMPLEX
Slot: Margin; May 27–June 18?; England
Role: To fulfill responsibilities to military and Free World
Cohesion: With military regulations
RC3.3.5; RE14, 16; G10-11

Class: FNS AND SMALL BOATS COMING TOGETHER COMPLEX
Slot: Margin; Early hours of May 27; Sheerness
Role: Because of concern for troops and British Empire
Cohesion: Same as for RC3
RC3.3.2; RE7b-8; G6-7.2

Class: GERMAN MILITARY DOES NOT WIPE OUT VAST ARMIES
Slot: Nucleus; By June 5; Dunkirk area
Role: Same as for RC3
Cohesion: Same as for RC3
RC3.3.4; RE15; G5.3, 10, 12.6, 13

(26) ACCOMPLISHMENT COMPLEX =

Class: CHANNEL CROSSING COMPLEX
Slot: Margin; Date same as for RC3.3.3; English Channel
Role: To get to Dunkirk
Cohesion: Same as for RC3
RC3.3.3.1; RE9-10; G7.3-4

Class: ARRIVAL COMPLEX
Slot: Margin; May 27–June 5; Dunkirk beaches
Role: To take troops off beaches
Cohesion: Same as for RC3
RC3.3.3.3; RE12; G8.2-11

Class: BEACH COMPLEX
Slot: Margin; May 27–June 7; Dunkirk area
Role: To gain control
Cohesion: Same as for RC3
RC3.3.3.2; RE11; G9

Class: SMALL BOATS ARRIVE AT A SAFE PLACE
Slot: Nucleus; May 27–June 5; British Isles
Role: Because they have escaped the Channel hazards
Cohesion: Same as for RC3
RC3.3.3.4; RE13; G11

(27) ARRIVAL COMPLEX =

Class: FIRST OF HUNDREDS OF SMALL BOATS PULL ON TO DUNKIRK SHORE
Slot: Margin; Same as for RC3.3.3
Role: (1) To rescue troops, (2) Because they have escaped hazards of the Channel
Cohesion: Same as for RC3
RC3.3.3.3.1; RE12a; G8.2
Note: An etic variant of this event might be [small boats pull onto shore].

Class: SOLDIERS CHEER
Slot: Margin; Same as for RC3.3.3
Role: Because they have hope of surviving
Cohesion: Same as for RC3
RC3.3.3.3.2; RE12b; G9.1
Note: An etic variant might be [soldiers express gratitude].

Class: AERIAL COMBAT DROWNS OUT CHEERS
Slot: Margin; Same as for RC3.3.3
Role: Because the combat is so very loud
Cohesion: Coherent with reality
RC3.3.3.3.3; RE12c; G9.1
Note: An etic variant might be [battle noise drowns out speech].

Class: SOLDIERS GET IN BOATS
Slot: Nucleus: Same as for RC3.3.3
Role: To escape
Cohesion: Same as for RC3
RC3.3.3.3.4; RE12d; G10.2, 11

(28) REPORT COMPLEX =

Class: OFFICIALS COUNT TROOPS WHO REACH SAFETY (Repeated)
Slot: Nucleus; Same as for RC3.3.5
Role: To account for personnel
Cohesion: Same as for RC3.3.5
RC3.3.5.1; RE14; G11

Class: OFFICIALS REPORT THE SAVING OF 338,266 BRITISH AND FRENCH TROOPS
Slot: Margin; Same as for RC3.3.5
Role: To let people (including Free World) know what has been accomplished
Cohesion: Same as for RC3.3.5
RC3.3.5.2; RE16; G11

(29) EVALUATION VECTOR =

Class: BN JUDGES WORK ON DUNKIRK BEACHES AS THEIR FINEST WORK
Slot: Nucleus; June 1940; British Isles, Channel, Dunkirk
Role: Same as for RC4
Cohesion: Same as for RC4
RC4.1; RE17; G13

Class: CHURCHILL COMPLEX
Slot: Margin; June 5–18; London?
Role: Same as for RC4
Cohesion: Same as for RC4
RC4.2; RE18–20; G12

Display 1.14 (cont.)

(30) CHURCHILL COMPLEX =

Class: CHURCHILL EXPECTS FUTURE GENERATIONS 1000 YEARS
HENCE TO JUDGE THE DUNKIRK MIRACLE TO BE
BRITAIN'S FINEST HOUR
Slot: Margin; Same as for RC4
Role: Because Britishers have done a courageous and honorable job
Cohesion: Same as for RC4
RC4.2.1; RE18; G12

Class: CHURCHILL SPEECH COMPLEX
Slot: Nucleus; June 18; London
Role: Challenge and commendation
Cohesion: Same as for RC4
RC4.2.2; RE19-20; G12

(31) CHURCHILL SPEECH COMPLEX =

Class: CHURCHILL CHALLENGES BRITISHERS TO DO THEIR
DUTY COURAGEOUSLY AND HONORABLY
Slot: Nucleus; June 18; London
Role: Because he is pleased with what Britishers have done, but they
must do a great deal more
Cohesion: With national unity and survival
RC4.2.2.1; RE19; G12

Class: CHURCHILL TELLS OF HIS EXPECTATION OF FUTURE
GENERATIONS
Slot: Margin; June 18, London
Role: To encourage Britishers
Cohesion: With national pride
RC4.2.2.2; RE20; G12

difficulty in an exclusively particle view in the analysis of data which in fact comprise a wave or continuum of activity. Degrees of marginality and nuclearity point up the wave nature of data.

Another instance of our indecision as to the nuclearity of two constituents is in Display 1.14, Formula 25 MIRACLE COMPLEX. We have designated both the third constituent ACCOMPLISHMENT COMPLEX, and the fourth constituent GERMAN MILITARY DOES NOT WIPE OUT VAST ARMIES, each as nuclear. The whole concentration of the battle is toward the latter happening perhaps pointing to its greater nuclearity. Actually the timing of both constituents is simultaneous—the saving of the troops, and their not being wiped out. From that point of view they are both nuclear. Grammatically as we suggested above we considered G11 which reports the number of lives saved as marginal to G10 which tells of the miracle continuing nine days and nights. In any case, much more study is required to make more valid generalizations for such special kinds of interrelations.

Not only is relative prominence a feature of slot in a referential tagmeme, but place in time and space is also relevant to slot. Such information is necessary to understand what is being said. Now we present role and cohesion—two more features of the tagmeme which are added to the formulas. We have discussed already the role of each single event but now we present the roles of larger structures in which those single events and their roles function. Also we include cohesion which speaks of constraint features which any part of the whole context imposes on the particular kind of event or sequence of events which may occur in any given tagmeme. Consider again Display 1.14, Formula 18. The role of the first constituent, GERMAN ATTACK VECTOR, is 'To dominate Europe.' Such a role is not specified in the text, but we have guessed that most of those involved would agree to that as an immediate goal of the German military. Yet the sequence of actual events was coherent with failure.

On the other hand the cohesion feature of the RESCUE VECTOR is success, and the vector's role is 'To save vast armies.' The EVALUATION VECTOR has the role 'To evaluate activities in relation to goals' and is coherent with the human need to judge activities in relation to personal and national values.

The roles of included structures are usually one phase of the role of the including structure. Note the roles of the three immediate constituents in Display 1.14, Formula 19 of the GERMAN ATTACK VECTOR: 'To diminish enemy shipping' and 'To wipe out vast armies' which are both part of the role of the including structure: 'To dominate Europe.' Note that the cohesion for each of the constituents of Formula 19 is coherent with the German national conquest plan. We assume that events within the sea, land, and air activities are determined within the constraints of overall national plans. We point out, however, that there may be contrast of these features between including and included structures. The LAND COMPLEX has two immediate constituents each of which is coherent with success despite the fact that they are within a structure two layers larger—GERMAN ATTACK VECTOR—which is coherent with failure.

The successive layered nuclei within the RESUCE VECTOR provide a good example of slot, role, and cohesion features being the same. It is the margins which introduce additional role features to the whole. Consider in Display 1.14, Formula 25 the first margin A MIRACLE BEGINS. Its role is 'Because people risk their lives to provide escape for trapped troops' and the next margin about the BN's coming together has the role of 'Because of concern for troops and British Empire.' The last margin REPORT COMPLEX has the role 'To fulfil responsibilities to military and Free World.' This is the only constituent to which we have attributed a cohesion more specific than for the others; it is coherent with military regulations, but of course within the larger coherency of success.

There is an especially interesting feature in Churchill's speech which we may not understand correctly. In Formula 31, Display 1.14, to the margin CHURCHILL TELLS OF HIS EXPECTATION OF FUTURE GENERATIONS we have attributed the role of 'To encourage Britishers.' But it may also have a satirical role. In the course of discussing the text with colleagues of various nationalities, it was two German colleagues, on separate occasions, who reacted visibly as they read . . . *if the British Empire and its Commonwealth last for a thousand years* . . . On inquiry we learned that they had understood Churchill to be making a satirical reference to the Thousand Year Reich spoken of by Hitler. Since that time, we have listened to a tape recording of that part of Churchill's speech. Our American interpretation of Churchill's British intonation is that he is contrasting *this hour* (a short period of time) with the many hours of a very long time. It is done by a moderate stress on *thousand*, with an extra heavy stress on *this* followed by a pause. For us the stress pattern would have had to have been different for him to be contrasting a British thousand years with a German thousand years. This, once again, points to the fact that understanding a stream of speech is from a personal experience and from one's own world view. Such is a cohesion feature of structure we discuss in section 1.3.6. PERFORMATIVE INTERACTION.

1.3.5 The referential levels of event and identity

For these levels we give only a brief sketch. Each event is made up of identities such as entities, actions, states, place, quantity (indicating how many identities are involved), etc. Display 1.15 is a tree diagram of a directional event and an attribute relation. Display 1.16 is a tree diagram of a state event and a place relation. The formulas for these are seen in Display 1.17. The DIRECTIONAL EVENT of SMALL BOATS ARRIVE AT A SAFE PLACE consists of the three identities SMALL BOATS, ARRIVE, and A SAFE PLACE. Actually *small boats* is an etic variant—a member of the paraphrase set—of the class BATHTUB NAVY. See Display 1.18. In Display 1.15 we give additional examples of attribute relations in BN. In Formula 32 the role for the boats is 'Moving entity,' of arriving is 'Directional movement,' and for the safe place is 'Target of movement.' All three of these are obligatory to the construction. There is no **arriving** without **something** doing the arriving and a **place** to arrive. The plural in **boats** indicates more than one boat entity. G8.2 speaks of hundreds of such entities.

The STATE EVENT of FREE WORLD SITS BY RADIO is also made up of three entities: FREE WORLD with role of 'Statant Entity,' SITS with role of 'State,' and BY RADIO with the role of 'Location.' We list additional examples of place relation in Display 1.16. Each constituent is obligatory in that there is no **sitting** without **something sitting** and **being** in some **location**. We have tentatively included **at** with **arriving** as implied by that activity in the DIRECTIONAL EVENT, whereas we have included **by** relational constituent with **radio** as constituents of a place relation. We make this distinction because **arrive** implies **from** and **to** with accompanying entities of both **source** and **target,** whereas we see **sit** as implying only **location** with alternate place relations such as **behind, in front of, underneath, above, inside,** etc.

In Display 1.18 we present a taxonomy of the members of the cast. Any term which does not appear in the text we have enclosed in square brackets. We list for each group or cast member its paraphrases with an indication of the place where each occurs in the text; paraphrase sets are variant manifestations of a single emic referential unit.

The class BATHTUB NAVY is the most interesting class in the text, not only because it is the hero, but also because it has the most paraphrases. These we have arranged in a very simple taxonomic array which points toward some componential factors of meaning.

Display 1.15 Referential Tree Diagram of a Directional Event and an Attribute
Relation on the Identity Level of the HISTORICAL MACRO EVENT (BN)

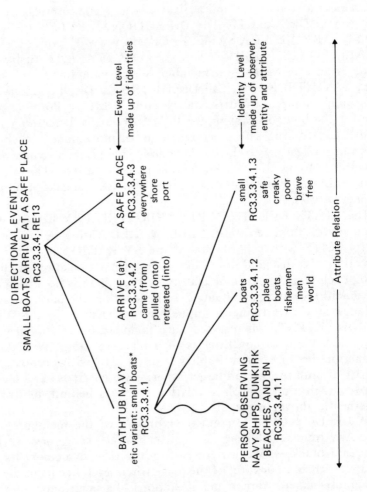

(DIRECTIONAL EVENT)
SMALL BOATS ARRIVE AT A SAFE PLACE
RC3.3.3.4; RE13

A SAFE PLACE ——Event Level
RC3.3.3.4.3   made up of identities
everywhere
shore
port

ARRIVE (at)
RC3.3.3.4.2
came (from)
pulled (onto)
retreated (into)

BATHTUB NAVY
etic variant: small boats*
RC3.3.3.4.1

small ——Identity Level
RC3.3.3.4.1.3   made up of observer,
safe   entity and attribute
creaky
poor
brave
free

boats
RC3.3.3.4.1.2
place
boats
fishermen
men
world

PERSON OBSERVING
NAVY SHIPS, DUNKIRK
BEACHES, AND BN
RC3.3.3.4.1.1

←———— Attribute Relation ————→

* Other variants (paraphrase set) of the class BATHTUB NAVY are to be seen in Display 1.18

Display 1.16 Referential Tree Diagram of a State Event and a Place Relation on the Identity Level of the **HISTORICAL MACRO EVENT**

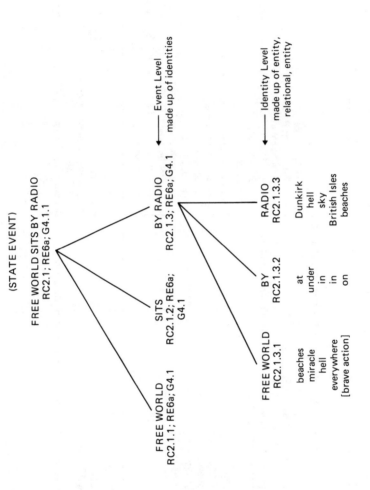

(STATE EVENT)

FREE WORLD SITS BY RADIO
RC2.1; RE6a; G4.1.1

FREE WORLD
RC2.1.1; RE6a; G4.1

SITS
RC2.1.2; RE6a;
G4.1

BY RADIO
RC2.1.3; RE6a; G4.1

⟵ Event Level
made up of identities

FREE WORLD
RC2.1.3.1

beaches
miracle
hell
everywhere
[brave action]

BY
RC2.1.3.2

at
under
in
in
on

RADIO
RC2.1.3.3

Dunkirk
hell
sky
British Isles
beaches

⟵ Identity Level
made up of entity,
relational, entity

⟵——— Place Relation ———⟶

Display 1.17 Referential Formulas for Event and Identity Levels of the HISTORICAL MACRO EVENT (BN): Formulas 32–35

Event Level:

(32) SMALL BOATS /BN/ ARRIVE AT A SAFE PLACE (DIRECTIONAL EVENT) =

Class: BN
Slot: Nucleus; Area of English Channel; May 27–June 5
Role: Moving entity
Cohesion: (1) Obligatory, (2) Characteristics coherent with entities which are able to move in a direction
RC3.3.3.4.1

Class: A SAFE PLACE
Slot: Same as for RC3.3.3.4.1
Role: Target of movement
Cohesion: (1) Obligatory, (2) Characteristics coherent with a place where moving entities could arrive
RC3.3.3.4.3

Class: ARRIVE (at)
Slot: Same as for RC3.3.3.4.1
Role: Directional movement
Cohesion: (1) Obligatory, (2) Movement coherent with entities able to move to the target.
RC3.3.3.4.2

Other examples of directional events:

Etic variant of BN class:	pull (onto)	the shore
small boats		
motley fleet		
creaky, beat-up fishing boats		
motor launches		
Tens of thousands of British and French troops	retreat (into)	the little French port of Dunkirk

(33) FREE WORLD SITS BY RADIO (STATE EVENT) =

Class: FREE WORLD
Slot: Nucleus; May 1940–June 5; In free world
Role: Statant
Cohesion: (1) Obligatory, (2) Characteristic coherent with state and location
RC2.1.1

Class: BY RADIO
Slot: Same as for first tagmeme
Role: Location
Cohesion: (1) Obligatory, (2) Characteristic coherent with specific statant and state.
RC2.1.3

Class: SITS
Slot: Same as for first tagmeme
Role: State
Cohesion: (1) Obligatory, (2) Coherent with entity and location
RC2.1.2

Identity Level:

(34) SMALL BOATS (ATTRIBUTE RELATION) =

Class: PERSON OBSERVING NAVY SHIPS, DUNKIRK BEACHES, AND BN
Slot: Nucleus, May–June 1940, England
Role: Evaluator
Cohesion: (1) Obligatory, (2) Coherent with personal judgment as to relevancy of attribute to entity in relation to context
RC3.3.3.4.1.1

Class: SMALL
Slot: Same as for first tagmeme
Role: Attribute
Cohesion: Obligatory
RC3.3.3.4.1.3

Class: BOATS
Slot: Same as for first tagmeme
Role: Entity
Cohesion: (1) Obligatory, (2) Coherent with characteristics of an entity which can have an attribute
RC3.3.3.4.1.2

Other examples of attribute relations:

fleet	motley
boats	creaky
place	safe
place	a
fishermen	poor
men	brave

(35) FREE WORLD BY RADIO (PLACE RELATION) =

Class: FREE WORLD
Slot: Margin? Before June 5; in free world
Role: Entity
Cohesion: Same as in Formula 33
RC2.1.1; RE6a; G4.1

Class: RADIO
Slot: Margin? Time and place same as for first tagmeme
Role: Entity
Cohesion: Same as in Formula 33
RC2.1.3.3; RE6a; G4.1

Class: BY
Slot: Nucleus; Time and place same as first tagmeme
Role: Position
Cohesion: Same as in Formula 33
RC2.1.3.2; RE6a; G4.1
Etic variants of BY class: beside, very near, at the side

Other examples of place relations:

beaches	at	Dunkirk
miracle	under	hell
hell	in	sky
everywhere	in	British Isles
[brave action]	on	beaches

Display 1.18 A Taxonomy of the Members of the Cast—Identities

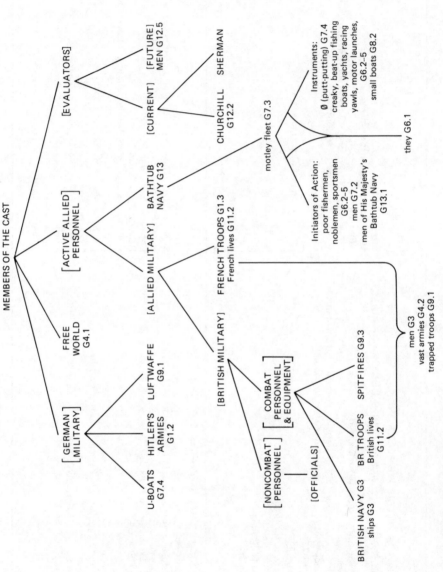

Note: Entries in lower case type are members of a paraphrase set.

Two terms: *motley fleet* G7. and *they* G6.1 refer to the total group, whereas other paraphrases refer to initiators of action while others refer to instruments of action.

We give only a sample of identity tagmemes; these we treat as the referential part of an entry in the Greater Lexicon:

(a) Initiators and patients of action
Class: TROOP (armies, soldiers, lives)
Slot: Nucleus
Role: Victim
Cohesion: With military characteristics of the Allies

Class: BATHTUB NAVY (for paraphrases see Display 1.17)
Slot: Nucleus
Role: Hero
Cohesion: With patriotic ideals, standard of bravery

(b) An entity of hypostasis
Class: MIRACLE (this, finest hour)
Slot: Nucleus?
Role: To save men
Cohesion: With unexpected good

We point out that the entity 'miracle' is a summary term for all that the Bathtub Navy did; it is hypostatizing all that activity, compacting all those higher level sequences into a single language conceptual entity. (A comparable entity of hypostasis raised from a lower level would be the entity 'beauty' which would summarize the common characteristics by which an evaluator considers entities to be beautiful.)

(c) Instrument
Class: RADIO
Slot: ?
Role: To transmit news
Cohesion: With current electronic technology

Note that the cohesion of identities, particularly apparent for members of the cast, has to do with their inherent nature and this controls the kinds of action of which that entity can be a part. In a novel an author develops the personality of a character to the extent that should he do anything out of character, the reader understands that something out of the ordinary has taken place. However, there are some characteristics so basic that only extreme trauma could alter them. Character traits, then, are features of an individual which key in to the coherence of all that he does (see Pike and Bernstein).

(d) Place entity: ENGLISH CHANNEL (water)
Slot: Margin; between France and Britain
Role: Traffic way; hazard
Cohesion: Cohesion with geography of actions

(e) A list of quantity of identities: We suggest quantity as indicating
the number of identities being referred to, whether one or many
identities.
tens of thousands troops G1.3; *few* ships G3; *vast* armies G4.2;
hundreds of boats G8.2; *nine* days and nights G10.2; [one] all
singular; [more than one] all plurals; *all* [hours] G13.1; *thousand*
years G12.4.

(f) Time: hour G5.2; morning G8.1; day G10.2; night G10.2; year
G12.4; all tense affixes.

Here we merely list a few more constituents (needing further
treatment) of the identity level, some of which could be entered in
one of the categories above: mines, guns, Free World, places such as
France, Dunkirk, Sheerness, all dates, empire and commonwealth
which are composite entities of animate, inanimate, geographical,
political line of command, etc.

Identities are frequently not the lowest level of the referential
hierarchy. Many of them consist of relations such as **attribute,
location, time, association, comparison,** and **of relations.** Some of
these may be seen in Displays 1.15 and 1.16, and Formulas 34 and
35 of Display 1.17. Others are simply listed below. We view these as
comparable to word level constructions in grammar;—in which
affixes may not occur without a stem. Attributes such as size, color,
beauty may not occur without some entity having that attribute,
as well as some person making such an evaluation of the entity. Also
place relations cannot be understood unless two entities are in relation to each other. Concerning attribute relations we have posited
three immediate constituents: entity, its attribute, and one who
judges the entity to have the attribute. Regarding this third constituent we are in some doubt as to the necessity of including it. In
Display 1.15 the wavy line from BATHTUB NAVY to PERSON
OBSERVING . . . indicates our doubt. In tagmemics the observer
is relevant at every point in the system. What is relevant about the
emic meaning of the word table is what the observer himself identi-
fies as *table*, not an etic abstraction which some might label 'table-
ness.' In regard to attributes, particularly those such as beautiful,
bad, tricky, etc., there will probably be much less uniformity of
judgement by different observers than for other referential consti-

tuents. Our question, then, is should such potential differences in judgement here, be made overt (or accessible to readers) by including that third obligatory constituent in ATTRIBUTE RELATION along with entity and its attribute. Our current judgement is affirmative.

We point out only one action that can be viewed as being modified by an attribute. That is the kind of fighting that Spitfires do in G9.3: *trying to fight them off* which means to us that the fighting was done with great effort against resistance. A modified action closer to its grammatical counterpart, but which does not occur in this text would be 'attack boldly.'

We simply list various kinds of relation constituents.

(a) Attribute Relations
   Size: *little* port G1.3; *small* ships G3, boats G8.2
   Power: *mighty* navy G3
   Mobility: *not agile* ships G3
   Behavior: *brave* men G4.2
   Wealth or Possessions: *poor* fishermen G6.2
   Use: *fishing* boats G6.3; *racing* yawls G6.5
   General: *Motley* fleet G7.1, [*very worn*] or *beat-up* boats G6.3
   Identity: *English* Channel G2
   Possession: *Hitler's* armies G1.2
   National Alliance: *British* troops G1.3, navy G3, or isles G6.1, or Spitfires G9.3, or lives G11.2, or empire G12.4, or Commonwealth G12.4, [*British* king] or His Majesty G13.1; *French* port G1.3, or lives G11.2, or troops G1.3; [*German* military] G7.4, or Luftwaffe G9.1
   Power Source: *motor* launches G6.5
   Mental State: *frustrated* Free World G4.1; *anguished* Free World G4.1
   Quality of Action: fighting with *great effort against resistance* in G9.3 *trying to fight them off.*
(b) Place Relation: Free World *by* radio G4.1; [brave actions] *on* beaches G13.4; beaches *at* Dunkirk G13.4; miracle *under* hell G10.1; everywhere *in* British Isles G6.1; hell *in* sky G10.1
(c) Time Relation: retreated *as* Hitler's armies G1.2; pulled *as* sun G8.1; retreated *on* May 26, 1940 G1.1; said *on* June 18 G12.1; began *in* early hours G5.2; set sail *by* moonlight G7.3; all past tense, continuing aspect (*ing*); future time (*will*) G12.5. (*let*) G12.3
(d) Association Relation: fishermen *with* boats G6.2–3; noblemen *with* yachts G6.4; sportsmen *with* yawls, launches G6.5; men *with* (*out*) guns, or uniforms G7.2
(e) Evaluator Relation: hour *for* men G13.1–2

(f) Comparison Relation: *first* of all members of motley fleet G7.1;
     first of all boats G8.2; great*est* of all honors G13.3; fin*est* of all
     hours G13.2; small, agile *enough* in contrast to boats that are too
     large to go in to beaches G3
(g) *of* relations:
     Multiplier *of* multiplicand: tens of *thousands* G1.3
     Entity composed *of*: armies of *brave men* G4.2; hundreds of
     small boats G8.2
     Part *of* whole: first of *fleet* G7.1; first of *hundreds* G8.2; first of
     motley fleet G7.1; finest hour of *all* [*hours*] G13.2; hours of
     May 27 G5.1
     Action *of* actor: cheers of *soldiers* G9.1; roar of *Luftwaffe*
     [*plane* and guns] G9.1; crackle of *Spitfires* [and *guns*] G9.3
     Entity identified *of*: miracle of *Dunkirk* G10.2
     Attribute *of* entity: hour of *honor* 'honorable' G13.3

1.3.6 Performative interaction

PERFORMATIVE INTERACTION is the referential counterpart to
the grammatical I-THOU-HERE-NOW AXIS, as embodied in the
communication exchange GC0.1 *I say something to you.* and GC0.2
I hear something from you. This is either implicit or explicit for
every stream of speech. The referential events of this exchange
between Sherman and the authors are to be found in RE21-24. The
tree diagram of them is found in Display 1.19, and the formulas are
in Display 1.20. These events involve Sherman's selection of the
Battle of Dunkirk as being a good subject for his article, and that the
BN judged their finest hour to be on the beaches of Dunkirk. Such
selection of events happened before he 'tells' about the macro event,
but no doubt some of the relevant facts of the battle were selected as
he was telling the story. The cohesion features of the events relative
to the speaker and hearer in the encoding and decoding process are
of particular interest. These are coherent 'with the very complex
personal, physical and psychological make-up, knowledge and use of
language, some of which is conscious, but most of which is subconscious,' of both the speaker and hearer. The authors' technical
analysis is 'coherent with the tagmemic model of communication.'
The role for that constituent is 'to account for some salient factors
contributing to their understanding of the Bathtub Navy.' We make
no claim to have verbalized all details of our understanding of the
text. Also each factor we have spoken of, especially role and
cohesion, merits considerably more study—and in some instance
very extensive studies.

Display 1.19 Referential Tree Diagram of the Speaker-Hearer Relationship in Space and Time; PERFORMATIVE INTERACTION

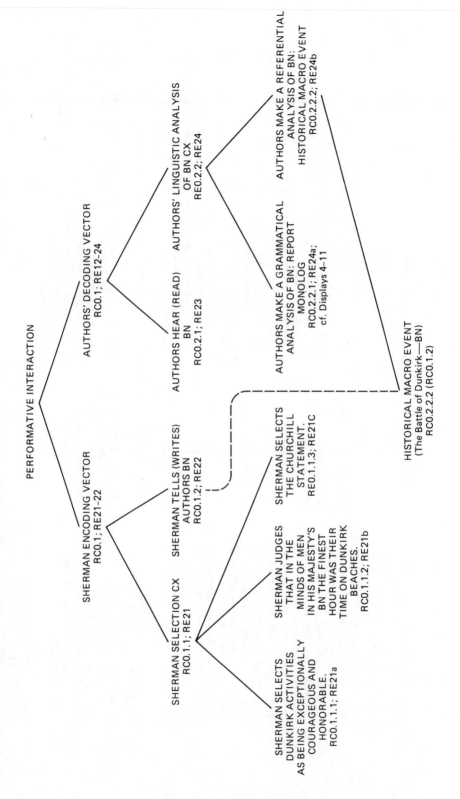

Display 1.20 Referential Formulas for PERFORMATIVE INTERACTION: Formulas 36–40

(36) PERFORMATIVE INTERACTION =

Class: SHERMAN ENCODING VECTOR
Slot: Nucleus (of PERFORMATIVE INTERACTION); Place unknown,
      authors' home* May 1971
Role: Because Sherman wants to say* something to authors
Cohesion: With Sherman's notion of what is appropriate to tell authors
RC0.1; RE21–22

Class: AUTHORS' DECODING VECTOR
Slot: Nucleus (of PERFORMATIVE INTERACTION); authors'
      home*; May 1971
Role: To receive pleasure and information
Cohesion: With kinds of people authors like to listen to
RC0.2; RE23–24

(37) SHERMAN ENCODING VECTOR =

Class: SHERMAN SELECTION CX
Slot: Place unknown; After June 18, 1940 and before and partially
      simultaneous with RC0.1.2
Role: Same as for RC0.1
Cohesion: With Sherman's evaluation of era
RC0.1.1; RE21

Class: SHERMAN TELLS (WRITES)* BN FROM HIS
       PERSPECTIVE.
Slot: Nucleus; Same place and time of RC0.2
Role: [To tell others (including authors) what he thinks is important
      relative to the miracle of Dunkirk.]
Cohesion: With Sherman's very complex personal physical and psycho-
      logical make-up, knowledge and use of language including phonology
      and grammar, some of which is conscious, but most of which is
      subconscious
RC0.1.2; RE22

(38) SHERMAN SELECTION CX =

Class: SHERMAN SELECTS DUNKIRK ACTIVITIES AS BEING
       EXCEPTIONALLY COURAGEOUS AND HONORABLE
Slot: Same place and time as for RC0.1.1
Role: [Because he is looking for incidents to interest and encourage
      people including authors (readers of Reader's Digest).]
RC0.1.1.1; RE21a

Class: SHERMAN SELECTS THE CHURCHILL STATEMENT
Slot: Same place and time as for RC0.1.1
Role: [To present context in which Sherman's judgement is validated.]
RC0.1.1.3; RE21c

Class: SHERMAN JUDGES THAT IN THE MINDS OF MEN IN HIS
       BN THE FINEST HOUR WAS THEIR TIME ON DUNKIRK
       BEACHES.
Slot: Same place and time as for RC0.1.1
Role: [Because he recognizes that it was there that occurred the peak
      of courageous and honorable action of the F, N, S.]
RC0.1.1.2; RE21b

(39) AUTHORS' DECODING VECTOR =

Class: AUTHORS HEAR (READ) BN
Slot: Nucleus; Same place and time as RC0.1.2
Role: Same as for RC0.2
Cohesion: With authors' very complex personal physical and
psychological make-up, knowledge, and use of language, some of
which is conscious, but most of which is subconscious
RC0.2.1; RE23

(40) AUTHORS' LINGUISTIC ANALYSIS OF BN CX =

Class: AUTHORS MAKE A GRAMMATICAL ANALYSIS OF BN:
REPORT MONOLOG
Slot: Nucleus; Juba, Sudan Dec. 1981–Jan. 1982; revised Jan.–Feb. 1983
Role: To verbalize some grammatical structure which contributes to the
understanding of BN
Cohesion: Same as for 0.2.2
RC0.2.2.1; RE24a; Cf. Displays 4–11

Class: AUTHORS' LINGUISTIC ANALYSIS OF BN CX
Slot: Margin; In various places 1974–1983
Role: To account for some salient factors contributing to their under-
standing of BN
Cohesion: With tagmemic model of communication
RC0.2.2; RE24

Class: AUTHORS MAKE A REFERENTIAL ANALYSIS OF BN:
THE BATTLE OF DUNKIRK
Slot: Juba, Sudan; Jan. 1982; revised Jan.–Feb. 1983
Role: To verbalize some referential structure which contributes to
their understanding of BN
Cohesion: Same as for RC0.2.2
RC0.2.2.2; RE24b; Cf. Displays 12–19

* For simplicity we have substituted the actions of writing, publishing, and reading with telling and hearing. This involves the hypothetical place of
the 'telling' as being the authors' home and in May 1971, the date of publication in *Reader's Digest*.

These factors of decoding include not only grammar and reference, but also phonology. If the phonology of the speaker and hearer differ widely, communication is impaired. Some time ago the authors attended an English lecture in a foreign country given by a local scholar speaking on a topic of deep interest to them. The phonology was so different from that of the authors that they understood very little, but what they did understand seemed to be very close to their grammatical and referential idiolect. The rest of the audience, which was a local group, seemed to understand the speaker readily; at least they laughed intermittently together and their interest seemed to be held. It is by all three structures of language that speech communication is achieved.

1.4 THE GREATER LEXICON

The greater lexicon, which includes not only entries of lower level constituents but also of all higher level constituents as well, is the interface of the three hierarchies. Each entry is identified as to its phonological class, its grammatical class, and its referential class. Currently in a dictionary entry the pronunciation represents the phonological class, the grammatical label (verb, noun, or other) represents the grammatical class, and the meaning represents the referential class. There is greater standardization of grammatical class labels than of phonological or referential class labels. Consider the grammatical class labels (1) for words: noun, verb, adjective, adverb; (2) for clauses: intransitive, transitive, bitransitive, equative; (3) for sentence: independent, dependent, condition-contingency, cause-effect.

The lexicon is an index for classes and the formulas of each hierarchy show the appropriate occurrence (distribution) of those classes. Any entry is a unit in one of the hierarchies, and most are units also in the other two as well, but some units are *not* also a unit in one or the other hierarchy. Consider the phonological word *I'm* in *I'm going*, which, although it is a simple phonological word, is a sequence of the two grammatical words *I* and *am*. Consider the *-o* in the Spanish word *hablo* 'I speak.' It is a single phonological unit (phoneme), as well as a single grammatical suffix (morpheme), but it is a fusion of referential units: first person, singular, present tense, indicative, and active voice.

We continue with higher level lexical entries: Consider the following proverb: *Birds of a feather flock together*. This has a literal meaning as well as a metaphorical meaning: (1) 'birds which have the same kind of feathers keep together in a group' versus 'people of the same character and interests attract each other.' Any statement that is accepted as a paraphrase of the literal meaning is a member of that referential class, even as a paraphrase of the metaphorical meaning is a member of a second referential class. Note that the substance of reference includes the happening about which we can speak—in other words for which we have a metalanguage relative to the memory of an actual happening, or imagination of something we expect to happen, or we imagine to have happened. The grammatical class of the 'bird' proverb is an independent, declarative, bi-intransitive clause root. The phonological class is some kind of a riming couplet.

A second proverb: *A stitch in time saves nine* is a phonological riming couplet, an independent declarative transitive clause root, and has both a literal and a metaphorical meaning. The term PROVERB is a composite (conflation or intersection) of all three structures, but probably the referential intent provides the most prominent intended component.

A limerick is a stream of speech which is a class (genre) which also can be defined as a special form of intersection of phonological class, grammatical class, and referential class. If any one of these features is not present, it is no longer a limerick. Its phonological class (excepting the riming pattern) can often be identified on nonsense syllables by at least half of the members of a class of native English speakers. These phonological features may be referred to as Phonological (P) Limerick class whereas the grammatical features can be referred to as (G) Limerick class, and the referential ones as (R) Limerick class.

Referential structure is primarily encyclopedic—having to do with the specific stream of speech and its paraphrases; hence multiple class membership particularly on higher levels is minimal, apart from taxonomic (or other) including structures. The conflation of many referential structures gives the lexical referential classes. For example, the name *Allan* as a lexical type entry is the name of a male, whereas the *Allan* who authored 'The Bathtub Navy,' is a specific individual —an encyclopedic type of entry.

We make note of the class meaning of some grammatical classes. Very well known are the correspondence of some grammatical affixal or pronominal referent systems between human versus non-human nouns, or between masculine entities and items used by males versus female entities and items used by females. However it is not so well known that the class of direct quotation may, among other things, signal a high social status of the person quoted versus the indirect quotation which may signal a person lower on the social scale. Also the latter may signal a quotation within a quotation such as (*he said that she said*) *that she would go*. Direct quotation without identification of speaker or addressee, normal to drama, may in a narrative signal the climax of the story. The grammatical form of a question may signal not only request for information, in one context, but in other contexts may signal an insult or challenge. Each of these meaning differences in speech must be accounted for.

The referential value or class of each entry would include its taxonomic relation to all other classes at its level. This would show its contrastive-identificational features. It would include its role and cohesion features, even as we have shown in a sketchy way for the classes: BATHTUB NAVY, TROOP; RADIO, etc., in Section 1.3.5.

The Battle of Dunkirk, a specific instance of HISTORICAL MACRO EVENT, is a nuclear event in the retreat of allied forces from Western Europe before the advance of the German offensive toward the south and west. Its role is the rescue of allied troops from the allied point of view, and to dominate more of Europe from the German point of view. It is the product of the authors' decoding vector; how close it is to Sherman's encoding product we do not attempt to determine.

Much of what has been done in the field of general semantics is relevant for us in the Greater Lexicon but will not be treated here.

1.5 SUMMARY

We have presented a sketch of the tagmemic analysis of grammar and reference of the BN text. These are factors involved in our understanding—exegeting—a stream of speech. Grammar is the structure of the text as it is told (or written); reference is the structure of the events in history which the stream of speech (or writing) is referring to. The analysis is hierarchical in that it presents structures layer by layer. Each structure is in contrast with all others; each has a range of variability; each occurs in appropriate, distinctive places. Each constituent of any construction is characterized by the four features of class, slot, role, and cohesion, answering the following questions respectively: what, where, why, and whence governed. This system of formulas together with lists of minimal classes (morpheme classes for grammar and relation or identity classes for reference) will predict appropriate streams of speech to a manageable degree of accuracy for our purposes. Many features we have touched on require a great deal more study; indeed a significant number of scholars are working in many of these areas and can fill in gaps in our description. See Longacre (1981), Grimes (1978), Halliday and

Hasan (1976), Van Dijk (1978), and others. However, this meta-language—along with metatexts—for discussing a stream of speech, provides a way of understanding and talking about many relevant features of language and communication.

Incidentally, if one criterion of truth is a coherency in system, consider the vast amount of data which tagmemics treats usefully and coherently. This gives us courage to believe that our system itself is not irrelevant.

2 Phonological Hierarchy in a Four-Cell Tagmemic Representation from Poem to Phoneme Class

Kenneth L. Pike

2.0 PURPOSE, DATA, AND APPROACH

The purpose of this analysis is to show that a poem, as a single unit, can be studied in relation to its internal structuring into successive constituents, for each of which its phonology can be given a four-celled tagmemic representation.

In 1974 Martin and Pike in an article entitled 'Analysis of the Vocal Performance of a Poem: A Classification of Intonational Features' analyzed many phonetic and phonemic features of pitch and voice quality of the selected poem on various hierarchical levels. In this present article, the author starts by taking some of that same data (see Display 2.1A) and utilizing it to illustrate some four-cell formulas to present in a more visible way the hierarchical structure of the poem, while emphasizing the theoretical importance of the tagmeme (i.e. of unit-in-context). The poem is 'Who But the Lord,' written by Langston Hughes, as read by Ossie Davis on a Caedmon record TC 1272. It is a poem about a black in the thirties, under unjust police attack in the U.S.A. The original article by Martin and Pike emphasizes phonological, digital, and analogical elements of the reading rather than providing four-cell formulas.

It mentions (in footnote 11) that 'A complete description of the phonological hierarchy would involve at least seven levels . . . phone, syllable, phonological phrase, phonological clause, phonological sentence, phonological paragraph, discourse.' I am discussing some of these here, via formulas.

The poem as a whole includes grammatical, referential, and phonological elements simultaneously present. Here we look principally at the poem as comprising a phonological discourse. As such, it has as its top hierarchical level a binary structure which is artistically and linguistically fascinating. The poem as originally published in *One*

Way Ticket in 1945 did not contain the last line. The last line now comprises a postmarginal unit by itself, in sharp semantic and phonological contrast to the nucleus of the original poem as a whole. This can be seen semantically as being the sole place where the poem seems to look to the future. Phonologically (which concerns us here) it is marked by the tentative pause—indicated by the single slash line (/) instead of by a final double slash (//)—which contrasts sharply with the final pause which ends Line 22. In general, the single slash indicates an unfinished statement, in contrast to the more relaxed finality of a final pause.

A four-cell formula, which we will use in a moment to represent this material, suggests that items must always be *seen in context*; hence there is presented a theoretical construct, a *unit-in-context* —called a tagmeme—which diagrams these relations. In the upper left-hand corner (Cell 1, see Display 2.2) is a representation of the *slot* (or place, or position) in which an item occurs in the immediately-larger unit which contains it; simultaneously, one often suggests that such an including unit is in the form of a *wave* with a nucleus, optionally preceded or followed (or both preceded and followed) by less important marginal elements leading up to or away from the nuclear peak or climax. In the upper right-hand corner (Cell 2) is the *class* of items (or class of classes of items) which are appropriate to occurrence in that slot of that kind of structure, illustrated in this particular instance by one member of the class; and such an item, in turn, is broken down into its own constituents in later formulas, until it reaches the minimum for that system. In Cell 3, at the lower left, one finds the role played by that unit-in-context; but here the relevance is its function which is *additional* to the *form* —i.e. which is a *semantic* component, or social relevance. In Cell 4, to the lower right, the context is of a still different kind: a *background system* containing that item or its relation to other items in the discourse which it controls or which are controlled by it; or a set of beliefs or expectancies which give an over-all coherence to the discourse (or part of it) in a unity of sanity, or sense, or formal consistency (or *field*), called, here, *cohesion*.

2.1 THE POEM DIVIDED INTO PARAGRAPH COMPLEX AND FINAL TENTATIVE PAUSE GROUP

In Display 2.3 the four-cell structure of the phonology of the poem-as-discourse—the poem as a whole—is seen as made up of two tagmemes. In the first tagmeme the content (Cell 2) is the body of

Display 2.1A A Poem by Langston Hughes, as read by Ossie Davis on Caedmon record TC1272; and marked for phonological characteristics by Martin and Pike (Markings are emic approximations.)

WHO BUT THE LORD?

K4, R4, I4,
V5, P4, St4

1. I looked and I saw /
2. That man they call the law. //
3. He was coming
4. Down the street // at me! //
5. I had visions in my head
6. Of being laid out / cold and dead, //
7. Or else murdered /
8. By the third degree. //

K3, R3, I4,
V4, P4, St3

9. I said, O Lord, / if you can, /
10. Save me from that man! //
11. Don't let him make a pulp / out of me! //
12. But the Lord / he was not quick. /
13. The law / raised up his stick /
14. And beat the livin' hell /
15. Out of me! //

K2, R2, I2,
V3, P2, St4

16. Now I do not understand
17. Why God don't protect a man /
18. From police brutality. //
19. Being poor and black, /
20. I've no weapon to strike back
21. So who but the Lord /
22. Can protect me? //

23.   We'll see. /

Display 2.1B

WHO BUT THE LORD?

I looked and I saw
That man they call the Law.
He was coming
Down the street at me!
I had visions in my head
Of being laid out cold and dead,
Or else murdered
By the third degree.

I said, *O, Lord, if you can,*
Save me from that man!
Don't let him make a pulp out of me!
But the Lord he was not quick.
The Law raised up his stick
And beat the living hell
Out of me!

Now I do not understand
Why God don't protect a man
From police brutality
Being poor and black,
I've no weapon to strike back
So who but the Lord
Can protect me?

We'll see.

Langston Hughes

the poem—all except the last line—in the form of a paragraph complex (i.e. a structured sequence of paragraphs). Cell 3 implies that the role of that paragraph sequence (*as indicated by its phonology*, not by its grammar or by its lexical meanings) is the gradual building up of tension (by devices which will become apparent when one gets to the notation of the lower levels, as in specific paragraphs in contrast to one another in Displays 2.4 and 2.5).

Cell 1 of the first tagmeme of Display 2.3, on the other hand, states that the paragraph complex referred to in Cell 2 is the major, nuclear part of the phonological discourse—which, similarly, we indicated in prose (rather than by formula) earlier on. Cell 4 suggests that the internal cohesion of the whole has come to an end, with prediction of final closure by use of a detached, unstressed phrase (Line 22) ending in final fade and pause (marked with double slash).

This sets the stage for a denial of closure by the second tagmeme (Line 23), which ends in the tentative pause marked with single slash.

Display 2.2 The Tagmeme, as a *unit-in-context*, rejects any approach to language which abstracts items from context under the assumption they can be understood in isolation from larger context, or by abstracted formal or logical internal description alone. Everything gets part of its nature *from its relation* to other items in the system. The relation includes that of the immediately-containing larger unit, the class of which it is a member, the impact on behavior or on the understanding of meaning which it elicits, and the coherence with a background with which it is integrated or by which it is controlled. Unintended loss of such controls may lead to nonsense, insanity, or error; deliberate flaunting of these controls may lead to irony, jokes, or lying.

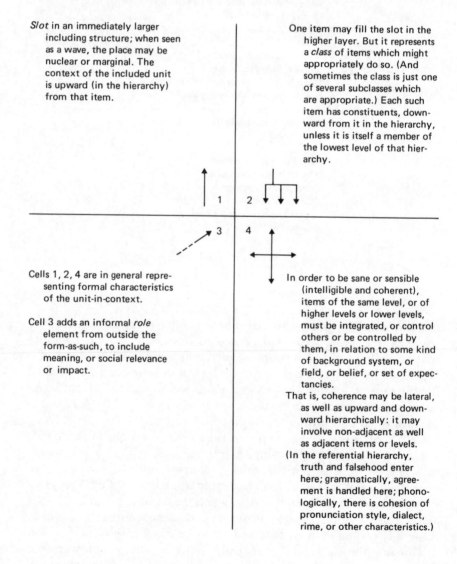

Slot in an immediately larger including structure; when seen as a wave, the place may be nuclear or marginal. The context of the included unit is upward (in the hierarchy) from that item.

One item may fill the slot in the higher layer. But it represents a *class* of items which might appropriately do so. (And sometimes the class is just one of several subclasses which are appropriate.) Each such item has constituents, downward from it in the hierarchy, unless it is itself a member of the lowest level of that hierarchy.

Cells 1, 2, 4 are in general representing formal characteristics of the unit-in-context.

Cell 3 adds an informal *role* element from outside the form-as-such, to include meaning, or social relevance or impact.

In order to be sane or sensible (intelligible and coherent), items of the same level, or of higher levels or lower levels, must be integrated, or control others or be controlled by them, in relation to some kind of background system, or field, or belief, or set of expectancies.

That is, coherence may be lateral, as well as upward and downward hierarchically: it may involve non-adjacent as well as adjacent items or levels.

(In the referential hierarchy, truth and falsehood enter here; grammatically, agreement is handled here; phonologically, there is cohesion of pronunciation style, dialect, rime, or other characteristics.)

Display 2.3 Immediate Constituents of the Poem as a Whole: the original poem (1945) comprises the nucleus of the phonological discourse, amplified later by the last line which may imply a hope or else an unspoken unactualized threat.

Phonological structure of the poem as a phonological discourse =	Discourse Nucleus	Paragraph complex	Discourse margin	Tentative pause group
	1	2	1	2
	3	4	3	4
	Building up of progressive tension	Implication, by final line (Line 22) in its unstressed, detached intonation, with fade to final pause, of closure to the whole poem	Unspoken implication of an incomplete afterthought	Noncohesive with the finality of the first tagmeme

This tentativeness (Cell 4) is in negative cohesion with the first tagmeme and lends surprise and power to the poem.

The second tagmeme of Display 2.3, is manifested (in Cell 2) by a single grammatical sentence which ends not with the 'normal' kind of 'period' in which the pitch falls to the lowest level while the intensity fades, but one in which the pitch falls quite low, but does not fade off in intensity as it reaches its low points. (Often, in fact, the pitch before tentative pause may fall less than usual, and at its lowest point continues level for a moment.) This impression is sharply heightened by the contrast with final pause ending the tagmeme just before it, at the end of Line 22; the contrast forces attention to the implication of the nonfinality of Line 23. Cell 1 of this second tagmeme of Display 3 claims that it is marginal to the discourse (supported for us by the fact of its later addition to the published poem). Cell 3 suggests that an implication of something yet to come is given explicitly by the tentative pause. This, in turn, is cohesive with the total discourse structure, comprising an afterthought (as claimed in Cell 4).

2.2 THE PARAGRAPH COMPLEX DIVIDED INTO PARAGRAPHS

But now we turn to the paragraph complex indicated in Cell 2 of Display 2.3, and show its internal structure, in its turn. This nucleus of the poem (i.e. all but the last line) is divided into three phonological paragraphs, which here are poetic stanzas. Judged by increasing key, rate, intensity, tenseness, and width of pitch interval, the last stanza is the nuclear phonological paragraph of the three. See Display 2.4, where the numbers from left to right, on all but the last row, indicate this increase from left to right (i.e. from five toward one).

The one exception, in Display 2.4, is that loudness (strength) reaches its peak in the middle stanza (i.e. 4, 3, 4). This leaves some indeterminacy, since that characteristic would lead to the analysis of the middle stanza as the phonological nucleus, if it were given analytical primacy. Why the difference? Perhaps a detailed study of the semantic content would show this: The report of the *event as such* reaches its climax in the middle stanza—and hence is nuclear from the point of view of content; but the author's puzzlement, and attempt to *evaluate* and *understand* the event, *later* reaches its climax in the final stanza. The event climax is signalled by loudness in this reading by Davis; the puzzlement climax is signalled by increase in rate and pitch. The general impact upon the reader (at least upon this reader) is that of loud complaint and outrage in the second paragraph (shown by loudness of phonology), but of uncertain puzzlement and plaintiveness shown in the third paragraph by the high tense but quieter style.

Display 2.4 Phonological Characteristics of the Paragraph, which comprise the three stanzas (and part two versus six of stanza two): Key (overall high to low, 1 to 5); Rate (fast to slow, 1 to 5); Intensity (strong to weak, 1 to 5); Vocal cords (tense to lax, 1 to 5); Pitch interval (wide to narrow, 1 to 5); Strength (loud to quiet, 1 to 5).

	Paragraph (Stanza) 1	Paragraph (Stanza) 2 a	b	Paragraph (Stanza) 3
Key	K4	K3	K2	K2
Rate	R4	R3	–	R2
Intensity	I4	I3	I2	I2
Vocal cords	V5	V4	–	V3
Pitch interval	P4	P3	–	P2
Strength	St4	St3	–	St4

Now, in Display 2.5, these materials combine with the representation of the three tagmemes of the paragraph complex (Cell 2 of the earlier four-cell display). The first two are treated as marginal (Cell 1, for each), the third as nuclear. The role (Cell 3) is progressively more intense, from detached anticipation, to dreaded involved development, to plaintive climax. The three paragraph tagmemes are tied together in a cohesive whole (Cell 4) by structural parallels (in terms of lines and rimes—see also Display 2.6); there is for each a similar structure of lines and rimes relating them in an *internal* cohesion system of *analogous structure*, while there is simultaneously a factor of *external* cohesion across the paragraphs, in the poetic repetition of the ending word *me* for the second and third of the paragraphs, riming with *degree* of the first (Lines 15, 22, 8). There is a further internal cohesion by analogy, in that each of the paragraphs has a relatively uniform internal phonological quality (suggested in Cell 2, and given in more detail in Display 2.6). Note that one kind of paragraph structure in this particular discourse is relatively easy to see because of the poetic characteristics of line and rime; but *voice quality types*, and *intonation structure can carry phonological paragraphing in prose, apart from any poetic special features.*

Display 2.5 The Paragraph Complex, from Cell 2 of Figure 2.3, is broken down into three paragraphs.

Paragraph complex =	Margin of para- graph complex	Para- graph 1 (low and slow quality)	Margin of para- graph complex	Para- graph 2 (medium quality)	Nucleus of para- graph complex	Para- graph 3 (more intense quality)
	1	2	1	2	1	2
	3	4	3	4	3	4
	Detached antici- pation	Internal cohesion of quality, line, and rime	Involved develop- ment	Cf. first tagmeme	Climax	Cf. first tagmeme

2.3 MARGIN AND NUCLEUS OF THE EMIC CLASS OF PHONOLOGICAL PARAGRAPHS

All of this implies a further breakdown of the paragraph itself into tagmemes which can in their turn be represented by four-cell formulas. We have reached a sharply new stage in the presentation and analysis, however. Up to this point we have had but a single illustration of each level of structure—just one poem (discourse) and just one paragraph sequence. This left no opportunity for the necessary attempt, in the study of the language as a whole, to find general (*emic*) formulas to *cover a variety* of such elements, with a single basic structure from which the variants depart (*etically*). Now, however, with three paragraphs of a somewhat similar type, we come closer to the basic goal; single formulas covering numerous examples which are the same structurally (emically), even though different (etically) in their detail.

At the same time, however, a further complexity arises. Thus far we have been talking as if the phonological structure were single, with a single set of non-overlapping high-level borders. But in fact there is more complexity than this. Rime may occur *within* a pause group, as for 'head' and 'dead' (Lines 5 and 6); or pause may interrupt a pair of riming lines (after Line 9 before 10, with 'can' and 'man'); or pause may interrupt a poetic line (as in Line 13 after the subject, or before a prepositional phrase as in Lines 4, 11, 15). Voice quality changes can come in the middle of stanzas (key and intensity, Line 12), or can characterize a single line (the prepositional phrase, Line 15, with its staccato quality). And structural intonation contours (shown by the unbroken solid lines) normally have at least one phrased stress in this analysis, reflecting the analysis of Pike (1945), but may occasionally be interrupted by pause, and resumed without intonational stress (Line 15).

We can treat riming schemes, intonation structured contours, and the voice quality as three subsystems of phonology. The vowel elements of the rime, and the line structures involving them, may be called *segmental* phonological structures; the intonational contours with their emic levels are *suprasegmental*; and the voice quality changes, or general changes, or the gradient analogic changes may be called *subsegmental*. See Pike (1963) for a diagram of the intersection of these three types of phonological structure.

All of these matters of rime, voice quality, and segmental type may affect phonological paragraphs, as we shall now see.

In Display 2.6 we give a tagmemic formula for the composite of various emic phonological paragraphs. Each is divided into two tagmemes. The first tagmeme is marginal, setting the stage for attention, and the second is nuclear, giving focus with the heightened involvement.

Display 2.6 A Phonological Paragraph Type (A Paragraph Eme), specific to this poem.

Margin		Nucleus	
	(a) Segmental, three-line riming section, as poetic section (subparagraph) (b) Suprasegmental (phonological sentence or sentence cluster) (c) Subsegmental voice quality		(a) Segmental, three-line riming section (subparagraph) with heightened subsegmental quality Phonological sentences or sentence clusters (b) Suprasegmental (c) Subsegmental voice quality

Phonological paragraph in = the poem	1	2		1	2
	3	4		3	4

Setting of stage. Riming role calls attention to referential tie (often unexpected) in good poetry between rimed lexical items	(a) With internal tie of first two lines by rime; external tie to next section, and to next paragraph by rime (or identical word) (b) Subdued in relation to heightening of nucleus	Heightened involvement	Cf. first tagmeme

2.4 CHARACTERISTICS OF CONSTITUENTS OF POETIC SUBPARAGRAPHS

Note, especially, in Display 2.6 the division in Cell 2 between (a) the segmental phonological riming sections, and (b) the suprasegmental phonological sentences, or (c) the subsegmental voice-quality units. Within the phonological paragraph here, the three types of data (a), (b), and (c) may sometimes give different internal divisions to the paragraphs. Division type (a) is here a special *poetic* segmental structure superimposed upon the *normal* phonological paragraph of type (b) or (c) in its various suprasegmental or subsegmental forms. There are three such phonological paragraphs in the poem: Lines 1-8, 9-15, 16-22 (i.e. excluding Line 23). We first look at these lines in relation to their poetic segmental structure (Display 2.7).

Lines 5-8 comprise the second poetic segmental phonological section (subparagraph) of the first phonological paragraph of the poem. In the section, Lines A and B (Lines 5 and 6 of the poem) rime (i.e. 'head' with 'dead'). But the complex section Line C-D (poem Lines 7-8) ends the complex with the word 'degree', riming

Display 2.7 The Poetic Section (subparagraph) breaks down into three tagmemes each manifested (Cell 2) by one structural poetic segmental line (or line complex). Lines A and B have mutual cohesion (Cell 4) by riming; Line C rimes with the comparable line of the two stanzas, giving phonological cohesion across the sections.

(a) Poetic phonological = + sections (subparagraph)

Margin		Segmental Line A		+	Margin		Line B		+	Nucleus		Line C (or C–D)	
1	2	1	2		1	2	1	2		1	2	1	2
3		3	4		3		3	4		3		3	4
Sets tension		Internal rimes, with Line B			Builds tension		Cf. Line A			Climax		Usually ends in an external rime identically with Line C–D of all other subparagraphs of the poem —but at least rimes with them	

Display 2.8 A Typical Phonological Sentence may be composed of tentative and final suprasegmental phonological clauses (emic pause groups).

(b) Typical phonological = sentence

Margin		Tentative suprasegmental phonological clause: . . . /		Nucleus		Finality phonological clause: . . . //	
1	2	1	2	1	2	1	2
3		3	4	3		3	4
Nonfinality		Prepares for nucleus		Finality		Fulfills margin	

with 'me' at the end line of the first section (Line 4); see also other section endings, with 'me,' in Lines 4, 11, 15, 22 but 'brutality,' with an unexpected stress—in relation to the author's own dialect —on the last syllable, in Line 18. Note, further, that this cohesive feature tying together the sections is also a cohesion feature tying Line 22 to the discourse nucleus (Lines 1-22)—i.e. tying the after-thought (second tagmeme of Display 2.3) to the paragraph complex (first tagmeme of Display 2.3); this segmental cohesion feature is in addition to that listed in Cell 4 of that second tagmeme of Display 2.3, ('see' of Line 23). Since the riming of Line A with B is within its containing section, we have labelled it *internal* cohesion. On the contrary, the rime of section Line C is *outside* its including section, since it is tied to another section in the same phonological para-graph—and then still further to the nucleus versus the afterthought of the poem as a whole. We have labelled this type of cohesion as *external* to the immediate constituents of the unit in which its manifestation occurs.

In Display 2.6(a), in Cell 2 of the tagmemes, we indicated that in addition to the division of a phonological paragraph into poetic sections by segmental means (i.e. by riming lines), that a different subdivision (b, c) could be induced simultaneously by suprasegmental devices. See Display 2.8 for the tagmemics of suprasegmental pause groups of the poem, and Displays 2.9 and 2.11 for the suprasegmental rhythm groups (intonational total contours), as constituents of those pause groups.

2.5 CONSTITUENTS OF THE PHONOLOGICAL SENTENCE

When, in the typical case, the tentative pause (shown by a single slash line) precedes the final pause (shown by a double slash), the first suggests incompleteness, and the second one finality. Optionally, more than one tentative pause may occur within the phonological sentence. Line 9, for example, contains two tentative pauses before the final one in Line 10. Line 11 contains both a tentative and a final one. As an *off-norm* instance, note that Line 23 contains only a tentative phonological clause—no final one occurs within that phonological sentence. (A final one may be there implied, but if so it is not stated—the hearer is left to supply it.) Similarly, off-norm options allow the final pause to precede the tentative one, for special effects—which are not listed in Display 2.8, nor illustrated in this poem.

2.6 CONSTITUENTS OF THE PHONOLOGICAL CLAUSE

The phonological clause in its turn is broken down into sequences of suprasegmental rhythm groups—see Display 2.9. A heavy-stressed rhythm group comprises the nucleus of such a clause; a rhythm group with normal stress supplies the margin to the phonological clause. The heavy stressed one gives emphasis (or primary *focus*). In general, furthermore, these stresses fall on syllables where lexical items (as normal phonological words) would normally have a stress. This gives an interlocking of normal, segmental (lexical) stressing with special suprasegmental (intonation-contour) stressing. When, however, the stress is off-norm, special stress may occur. (We may normally, for example, say 're-íterate'—but, as off-norm, 'ré-iterate' if we wish to emphasize the 're-'.) Notice that various differences related to stress placement may separate the author's personal dialect from that of the reader of the poem. For example, in Line 18 the author would have had stresses only on the second syllable of 'police' and 'brutality.'

Display 2.9 A Typical Phonological Clause (emic pause group) containing two (or more) suprasegmental phonological phrases (rhythm units), one with stronger stress than the other (or others).

	Nucleus		Heavy-stressed (˝) suprasegmental rhythm group (phonological phrase)	Margin		Normal-stressed (´) rhythm group (phonological phrase)
A typical phonological = clause		1 3	2 4		1 3	2 4
	Primary focus (emphasis)		Stress interlocking with normal placement expected on lexical items. Ties the syllables into a coherent rhythm unit. Controls intonation breaks between rhythm units.	Normal attention. Secondary focus		Cf. Nucleus

In addition, Line 9 begins with an optional off-norm form of pause group with a *weak rhythm unit* containing no emic phrasal stress (since the normal phonological-word stress of 'said' is suppressed). Various other off-norm forms in the poem demonstrate the substantial flexibility of the system as a whole. Note, for example, Line 19 with three rhythm units, each with normal phonological-phrase stress—i.e. none also with heavy phonological-clause stress.

2.7 RHYTHM GROUPS AND THEIR CONSTITUENTS

In Display 2.10 we go one step further down the phonological hierarchy: the rhythm groups of Cell 2 of the tagmemes of Display 9 are broken down into obligatory nucleus (primary intonation contour) and optional premargin and postmargin. The primary contours are stressed.

Frequently, the phonological phrase (rhythm group) is composed only of a primary contour, as seen in 'Save me' (first half of Line 10), or 'raised up' (middle of Line 13), 'From' (first word of Line 18), 'Being' (first word of Line 19). The primary contours differ radically in meaning, depending upon their internal structure (for which see discussion of Display 2.11).

Contrastive pitch levels are significant within nucleus and margins of the primary contours. High level is shown in Display 2.1 by a solid line just above the letters; mid pitch by a line just below them; low pitch by a line lower still; and extra-high pitch by a line substantially above the letters, above the line for high pitch.

In the precontour, mid pitch carries little meaning—it is relatively neutral as in 'He was' (Line 3), 'Of being' (Line 6). A low precontour before a mid-primary contour is similarly neutral, as with 'I' (Line 1), and 'By the' (Line 8). High precontour adds intensity, as in 'So who' (Line 21). Extra high precontour carries extra intensity—not seen in Display 2.1.

Occasionally a pause interrupts the primary contour, but if the basic intonation pattern of the primary contour is continued after the pause (with no primary stress starting a further primary contour), the interrupted ending may be called a *postcontour*. See 'at me' (Line 4), 'Out of me' (Line 15), and 'Can protect me' (Line 22). Note, further, that these last two instances are preceded by final and tentative pauses, respectively—providing an instance where suprasegmental phonological phrases (rhythm groups, intonation total contours) are interrupted by the off-norm presence of borders of the suprasegmental pause groups (see Display 2.6, Cell 2, subdivisions (a) and (b). Compare, for grammar, a phrase embedded in a word).

Turning now to the suprasegmental primary contour itself (the nucleus of the total intonation contour), we see in Display 2.11 that it must begin with a stressed syllable (or with the first part of such a syllable if the entire primary contour has occurred on that one syllable alone). For primary contours of two syllables in length, see, for example, 'visions' (Line 5), 'murdered' (Line 7); for three-syllable primary contours see '-tect a man' (Line 17), and 'but the Lord' (Line 21); for a five-syllable primary contour see 'Don't let him make

Display 2.10 The Suprasegmental Phonological Phrase is broken down into a nucleus which is optionally preceded and followed by margins. The nucleus provides the primary semantic component, and the basic control of rhythm timing.

Suprasegmental phonological phrase (rhythm group, total intonation contour) = ±	Margin	Class of precontours	Nucleus	Class of primary contours	Post-margin	Class of resumed contours. Postcontour
		+	+	±		
		1 2 / 3 4		1 2 / 3 4	1 2 / 3 4	1 2 / 3 4
	Secondary semantic component of attitude	Tied to rhythm group. Controls shortening of syllables. Carries contrastive pitch sequences	Focus. Primary semantic component of attitude	Controls basic rhythm sequence. Controls intonation breaks. Controls syllable lengthening	After-thought	Controlled in pitch by nucleus. Without phrasal stress

Display 2.11 The Primary Contour. The normal suprasegmental primary intonation contour with primary stress on its first (emic) syllable (or first part of the syllable), followed by a final syllable (or end of syllable), and with optional media-margin pitch movement supplying the major contrastive classes of pitches at these points combined into significant semantic intonation signals, and comprising the major timing feature of rhythmic sequences.

	Nucleus	Class of stressed emic syllables, or first part of syllable. Double-stressed syllable sequence	Margin	Change-point class of syllables, or part of syllable, or phonological word	Margin	Class of final syllables, or end of syllable
Suprasegmental normal primary intonation contour =		1 | 2		1 | 2		1 | 2
		3 | 4		3 | 4		3 | 4
	Attention point. Contrastive feature of contour	Obligatory. Controls rhythm timing. Pitch related to over-all system. Lengthens its stressed syllable	Contrastive feature of contour	Optional. Pitch related to system, involving fall-rise, or rise-fall	Contrastive feature of contour	Obligatory. Pitch related to over-all system. Fade of stress

a' (Line 11); for a six-syllable primary contour see 'I've no weapon to strike' (Line 20). For single-syllable primary contours, however, see —among many—'looked' and 'saw' (Line 1), 'call' and 'Law' (Line 2), 'Down' and 'street' (Line 4), 'head' (Line 5).

The primary contour of the phonological phrase is the central, most important carrier of contrastive, emic semantics in the English intonational system. Primary contours may differ radically from one another in meaning. In general, those which have falling pitch (sliding or stepping down) suggest focus or attention on the word or phrase which is stressed; see 'visions' and 'head' (Line 5), 'murdered' (Line 7), 'Save me' (Line 10), 'raised up' and 'stick' (Line 13), 'Being,' 'poor,' 'black,' (Line 19). The contours which are rising, on the other hand, in general imply that something is incomplete, or that something is to follow; see 'me' (Line 11), 'stick' (Line 13), 'back' (Line 20), 'we'll' (Line 23). Level primary contours in general imply that something that is important has been left unsaid; see 'black' (Line 19).

Within a somewhat long phonological-phrase primary contour, however, there may be further complications. Although this long unit carries the meaning, and is in part identified by its primary phonological-phrase stress, the primary contour may include one or more lexical words with a slight (partially suppressed) secondary subsidiary phonological-word stress which, in our analysis, does not enter the semantic system as described here and in Pike (1945: 73, 87). Yet it does in some sense affect the rhythm. Specifically, in a poetic line for formal metrical verse, these subsidiary phonological-word stresses may count toward the setting up poetic *feet*. That is, they are part of the internal segmental structure of the poetic seg-mental line, but not part of the suprasegmental identificational components of the semantically-relevant intonation contours. Note, in this poem, secondary stress marked on items such as 'un-' (of 'understand' of Line 16, or 'weapon' and 'strike' of Line 20). These give subsidiary contours. Here, once more, the segmental line and the suprasegmental intonational system may have crisscrossing elements. And the subsidiary contours, in general, will be deter-mined in part by the normal lexical placing of phonological-word stress—as is the normal primary stress placement of the primary contour of the phonological phrase; this, then, is an *interlocking* of phonological structures with lexical structures and with poetic structures.

We have indicated that glides can occur on single syllables—note the two-way glides on 'head' (Line 5), 'third' (Line 8), 'can' (Line 9), '-stand' (Line 16). These glides in general occur that way when the primary contour is entirely contained within that one syllable. But occasionally, for special attention, the glide falls on the first syllable of the contour, and the contour finishes on a lower (or higher) level; see the glide on 'Save' (Line 10, with primary contour being 'Save me'), or 'Don't' (Line 11).

Our notation requires a gliding indication on the syllable in such cases. When there is a *gradual* stepping down to the ending syllable, our notation distorts that fact by showing a step down right after the first syllable; as 'I've no weapon to strike' (Line 20).

All these primary contours are important in relation to the total contour with its precontours. In general, the total contour, in ordinary speech, takes the same time as a primary contour by itself; the whole is speeded up (especially the precontour) so as to allow relatively uniform recurrent timing of such total contours. But here, again, there may be clash with a poetic segmental formal type: in normal speech it is the total contour which comprises the timing unit, whereas in *metrical* poetic form (not shown here) it may be the time of an arbitrary division from stress (primary or subsidiary) to stress plus a specified number of syllables which may belong wholly to either the first or the second contour, or split between the two. Here, once again, the segmental poetic line structure may crisscross with the suprasegmental speech norm.

Display 2.11 shows, further, that the nucleus of the primary contour can be comprised of two syllables each of which is stressed (cf. a spondee). Note, for example, the difference between the double-stressed 'That man' (Line 2) versus single-stressed 'they call' and 'the law' in Line 2. See, also 'laid out' (Line 6), 'that man' (Line 10), and 'police' (Line 18).

2.8 SYLLABLE STRUCTURE

We now wish to move down to the consideration of the emic syllable patterns themselves. Many problems await us, however. We lack, for example, the help of the intonational meanings of the primary contours or precontours to aid in the decision as to contrasting syllable types; criteria are therefore limited to more formal features. This leaves more indeterminacies of analysis, of a kind troublesome to linguists in the forties when they wished to decide whether the 'ch' of 'chose' was one phoneme or a sequence of two; or whether the 'p' of 'poor' was a single aspirated phoneme or a sequence of stop phoneme plus the phoneme of aspiration; or whether the syllabic of 'out' was a single vowel, or a cluster of vowels /a/ plus /u/, or whether it was rather a cluster of the vowel /a/ plus the consonant /w/. From the same era, the question arises again as to whether or not one should use grammatical criteria (grammatical prerequisites) in the analysis.

For the analysis here, I have chosen, on the basis of convenience, simplicity, and coherence with the hierarchical view to treat the 'ou' of 'about' as a *complex syllable nucleus*, composed of the two vowels /a/ and /u/ with the first nuclear, in its turn, to the vowel cluster; the marginal /u/ is raised above the line in the notation /a^u/ to show its dependency on /a/. (The alternative, to treat the cluster as nuclear, but the second part as /w/, postpones the difficulty until one must decide what the postsyllabic clusters are; then one would have to split off the /w/ from the /t/ of 'about.')

Such problems lead us to a consideration of an interlocking list of criteria for *nuclearity* versus *marginality*:

(a) We wish to preserve *hierarchial integrity*, by applying a single set of principles repeatedly at different levels. For example, we utilize the principle of nuclearity both for the syllable as a whole (to show the vowel as nuclear to the syllable as a whole), and for the vowel clusters within it (with /a/ being nuclear to the vowel cluster). Similarly, we utilize the same basic principle for allowing the 's' to be marginal to the 'tr' of 'street' (Line 4), and for the 'r' to be marginal, in its turn, to the 't' in that same cluster, so that 't' is nuclear to the 'tr', which in turn is nuclear to the 'str', which in its turn is marginal to the syllable 'street', which then is nuclear to the total rhythm contour 'the street' (Line 4). (The only extensive discussion of such syllable-structure hierarchy known to us is in Pike and Pike (1947).)

(b) We wish to preserve grammatical integrity, when it is not in conflict with other criteria. An immediate-constituent break is postulated as coming between morphemes, rather than within a morpheme, when the choice is relevant and possible. Thus, in 'understands,' we might set up the 's' as marginal to the 'nd' (of 'stands'); this we consider preferable to making the 'n' marginal to a hypothetical nuclear 'ds' there.

There has been phonemic debate about the use of grammatical criteria (pre-requisites) in phonemic analysis. Bloomfield, however, used grammatical elements in the description of the distribution of consonants in relation to vowels and syllables in monosyllabic morphemes, polysyllabic morphemes, and in words of more than one morpheme. See, for example, Bloomfield (1933: 131–34), with restatement of the distribution in terms of emic classes, by Pike (1955: Vol. II, 1967: 330–38, Section 8.63); and see Bloomfield (1935), on vowel distribution in relation to sounds and to the shape of morphemes and words.

(c) Classes are more readily judged to be emic, i.e. structurally relevant to some particular nuclear or marginal slot within the syllable structure, if they can be seen to be describable as comprising a set of sounds each of which shares one or more articulatory features. For example, only the stops /p, t, k/, voiceless ones, occur in initial consonant clusters between the 's' and 'r' of words like 'spray,' 'street,' 'sky.'

(d) Random gaps in an otherwise systematic articulatory emic set according to (c) may usually be ignored in setting up an emic class according to the nuclear or marginal slot (or slots) which it fills. The fact that initially in syllables all consonants occur except 'h' and /ž/, and all occur finally in syllables exept 'ng' (as in 'hang' but not 'ngah') does not prevent us from treating both the set of initial single consonants and set of final single consonants as being members of the same basic emic set, the Consonant Class 1 (i.e. $/C_1/$). The subclasses with the gaps in them are *alloclasses* (etic classes conditioned by position). For an extensive listing of such alloclasses, based on the work of Bloomfield (1933), see Pike (1967: 330-38).

(e) If two classes of consonants occur next to each other in a cluster, the class with the largest set is usually best treated as nuclear, whereas the smaller set is marginal. For example, since /s/ is the only sound in the class preceding /tr/, it is marginal to that /tr/. When no consonant follows the stop, however, /s/ may be followed not only by /p, t, k/ but also by other consonants— so the /s/ is still marginal. As for initial clusters whose emic class contains /tr/, the second, marginal, member is part of a small class including the liquids /r, l/ and the semivowel /w/, as in 'clay,' 'crow,' and 'quick.' The first—nuclear—class includes the voiced and voiceless stops /b, d, g, p, t, k/, in addition to the voiceless fricatives /θ, f, s, š, h/, as—with /r/—in 'bray,' 'dray,' 'gray,' 'pray,' 'tray,' 'crow,' 'fray,' 'three,' 'shrink'; but with /l/ one has only 'blue,' 'glue,' 'play,' 'clay,' 'flew,' 'slew'—lacking the initial clusters /dl, tl, θl, šl, hl/; similarly, with /w/ one lacks /bw, pw, fw, šw/. Nevertheless, it is convenient to label the emic cluster as $/C_1(C_2)/$, in which the parentheses enclose the margin.

(f) Nuclearity in reference to the syllable as a whole, or subnuclearity within nucleus or margins of the syllable, is related to a general theoretical principle affecting to some extent all languages, as a human universal: we start with the definition that *rank of stricture* gives highest rank to *greatest degree of closure*. A stop ranks higher than a fricative; a fricative higher than a nasal or liquid; a nasal higher than a vowel; so that /t/ outranks /s/, /s/ outranks /n/, and /n/ outranks /a/. Many more details are involved, but it does not seem appropriate to discuss them here; for more complete presentation, see Eunice Pike (1954), with partial summary in Kenneth Pike (1967: 329-31.) The *lowest* rank will in general be *nuclear* to the *syllable*, i.e. the *syllabic*, with the high ranks marginal to the syllable. Exceptions, such as syllabic nasals, will be covered by an overriding principle (g). This sets the universal expectancy of *some* kind of etic syllable structure for every language, to be modified emically for such languages and with possible skipping of the syllable level in a rare instance; for Bella Coola as represented by Newman, see Pike (1967: 420-21). This relationship sets up the *wave characteristic* underlying most syllable structure, i.e. except for elements covered in (g). In general, we will for this article—subject to revision as more is learned about the topic—give general priority to the criterion of *prominence* derived from rank, even though it may be overridden in specific instances under pattern pressures of various kinds.

(g) Prominence may be given to some sound by stress, length, or pitch which leads it to be syllabic, overriding prominence derived from rank of stricture. That is, there may be syllabic consonants such as the final /n/ of *button* (but in English the analysis phonemically—as in our treatment here—may break it into a vowel plus consonant). In less normal situations, where no vowel or sonant occurs, a fricative may become syllabic, as in the exclamation 'pst!'; or there may be syllabic fricatives in very rapid speech where one or more vowels of a rhythm group are made voiceless.

(h) The number of levels of *immediate-constituent structure* needed for convenient description of any one language can be studied, similarly, in relation to a list of criteria. This is best discussed and illustrated for numerous languages by Eunice Pike (1976: 46–48): (1) A level may be needed 'as an environment for conditioning units of a lower level,' or (2) for conditioning features of that same level; or (3) to allow one to show readily that two or more unit types contrast on that level; or (4) to be used 'as a distributional matrix' for describing lower levels. When scholars differ as to the number of levels needed in such an analysis (because of indeterminacy in the system itself, involving irregularity in that system, or because of 'non-uniqueness' of description possibility from the viewpoint of the scholars involved), we need not be too disturbed. If two or more descriptions are *mechanically convertible* from one to another by a simple set of rules, either of them may be found to be useful; but we would personally prefer to choose the one which to us seems most perspicuous, and which we guess is psychologically most natural, or one which best serves practical purposes of literacy.

Against the background of this theory of syllable structure as depending upon prominence-derived-from-articulatory rank, overridden at times by suprasegmental ranking of prominence, but leading to levels of immediate constituents, we now turn to the presentation of a partial and tentative analysis of the emic syllable structure of English, as shown by our four-cell tagmemic notation. Occasionally, also, we suggest (5) that one must choose between postulating a further emic class of sounds, or a further phonological construction, or a further constituent level, based on the criterion that one decision is slightly less awkward than the other (even though either one of the options leads to an irregularity which is a nuisance).

Display 2.12 presents one emic syllable pattern where nucleus and margins are determined by the criteria listed above. The nucleus for the syllable *as a whole* is marked by the presence of vowel classes —i.e. by sounds of lowest rank—according to (f). Presence of any stresses or vowel lengths within these syllables reinforces this judgement, in line with prominence, related to (g).

Display 2.12 The English Emic Syllable Pattern {CVC}, with final consonant or consonant cluster obligatory to allow for the full class of permitted vowel types.

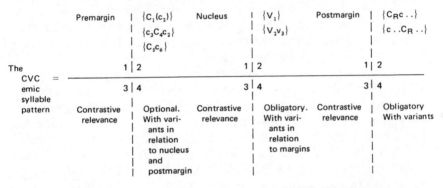

	Premargin	$\{C_1(c_2)\}$ $\{c_3C_4c_2\}$ $\{C_5c_6\}$	Nucleus	$\{V_1\}$ $\{V_2V_3\}$	Postmargin	$\{C_Rc..\}$ $\{c..C_R..\}$
The CVC emic syllable pattern =	1 | 2	3 | 4	1 | 2	3 | 4	1 | 2	3 | 4
	Contrastive relevance	Optional. With variants in relation to nucleus and postmargin	Contrastive relevance	Obligatory. With variants in relation to margins	Contrastive relevance	Obligatory With variants

The consonants, on the contrary, are marginal, in accordance with (f) but in reverse relation to the syllable wave since they have higher rank than the vowels. Display 2.13 shows this syllable wave in a simple idealization.

Display 2.13 A Wave-like Diagram of the Syllable results if the lowest rank of stricture (the vowel) is given highest place on the line superimposed on the syllable, with the syllabic as the peak (the nucleus) of that phonological wave.

C V C

2.9 CLASSES AND SEQUENCES OF VOWELS

Any of the vowels (set V_1) or monosyllabic clusters of vowels may occur in such a closed syllable (in our phonemic notation): /i/ 'street' (Line 4), /ι/, 'quick' (Line 12), /e/ 'laid' (Line 6), /æ/, 'man' (Line 10),

/a/ 'not' (Line 16), / / 'call' (Line 2), /o/ 'cold' (Line 6), / / 'looked'
(Line 1), /u/ 'boot,' /ə/ 'but' (Line 21); and the clusters (again, in
our phonemic analysis) /aⁱ/ 'white,' /aᵘ/ 'down' (Line 4), /ɔⁱ/ 'coin.'
(Evidence for this interpretation, phonemically, of phonetic diphthongs as implicit in the notation here is found in Pike (1947): for
example, monolingual American students of phonetics find it difficult to pronounce nondiphthongized /o/ or /u/ satisfactorily in—
say, Japanese—or even to hear that they are dipthongizing when
told that by such speakers; in addition, there is often loss of much of
the phonetic diphthongization in rapid pronunciation in rhythm group
precontours for /i, e, o, u/ but not, in those positions, for /aⁱ, aᵘ, ɔⁱ/.)
   In contrast with closed-syllable emic {CVC} (see Display 2.12), the
open-syllable pattern of emic {CV₄} has a more restricted set of
vowel types. Only the 'heavy' vowels and dipthongs /i, e, a, u, o, ɔ,
aⁱ, aᵘ, ɔⁱ/ can occur as the *stressed* nucleus of a *monosyllabic* morpheme when that syllable is *open*. Note /i/ 'me' (Line 11), /e/ 'Save'
(Line 10), /a/ 'pa,' /ɔ/ 'saw' (Line 1), /u/ 'do' (Line 16), /aⁱ/ 'I'
(Line 16), /aᵘ/ 'now' (cf. Line 16); but not the 'light' vowels /ɪ, ɛ,
æ, ɔ, v, ə/ in these open stressed vowels of monosyllabic words. On
the other hand, some of these may be found in open syllables of
dissyllabic words: cf. /ɪ/ in 'visions' (Line 5), /ɛ/ 'weapon' (Line 20),
/æ/ 'brutality' (Line 18), /o/ 'protect' (Line 22), /ə/ 'coming' (Line 3).
   Within the English syllable nucleus there is a further immediate
constituent layer, below the syllable as such, in which the first vowel
of a diphthong is nuclear to the diphthong as a whole. In our
phonemic writing, above, we indicated this by items such as /aᵘ/ in
which the second (nonnuclear) vowel is raised. In the nucleus of the
syllable pattern of Display 2.12, however, we did it by using an
upper-case letter for the nucleus, but a lower-case letter for the
margin, as in {V₂v₃}, where V₂ represented the list /a, ɔ/, and v₃ was
/i, u/ (or, in some dialects, /ɪ, v/). An irregularity restricts /ɔ/ so that
it is followed by /i/ but not by /u/; this would be shown in the
details of the cohesion cells, if we were to carry the four-cell notation down to that diphthong level here.
   In premargin, nucleus, and postmargin of the emic syllable {CVC}
the role (or function) of these constituents of the syllable is to
contrast one morpheme from another: /blæk/ 'black' (Line 19) in
premargin is not the same word as /bæk/ 'back' (Line 20); /hæd/
'had' (Line 5), in nucleus is not /hɛd/ 'head' (line 5); /aᵘt/ (line 6)
in postmargin is not /daᵘn/ 'Down' (Line 4). Similarly, on the next
lower level of immediate constituents, that of the nucleus of the
syllable, the members of the class of vowel clusters of V₂v₃ are
contrastive: /baᵘt/ 'bout' differs from /aⁱ/ /baⁱt/ 'bite.'

2.10 CLASSES AND SEQUENCES OF CONSONANTS

Turning again to Display 2.12, we note that in the premargin tagmeme Cell 2 (the class cell) has within it three alternative emic classes of consonant clusters which may serve as premargin there. Each of them, in its turn, needs a four-cell tagmemic representation; and each of them has its many variants and restrictions (*alloclasses* or *alloconstructions*) which would be in part suggested in the cohesion cells of the breakdown formulas. In addition, there is an astonishingly complex list of restrictions relating the consonants. We have indicated that Bloomfield discussed consonant distributional restrictions in relation to his aim (1933: 130) to 'show that no two of them [the phonemes of English] play exactly the same part [in distributional co-occurrence relations];' and his various subsets and restrictions are re-charted, to show etic subclasses, in Pike (1967: 331-8); we will not repeat that data here. Similarly, Bloomfield (1935) discussed for Chicago English the stressed vowels, and their massive distribution restrictions in relation to monosyllables, to polysyllables, to morphemic boundaries, and to consonants. Anyone who has not looked at such data in detail can hardly imagine the intricacies of the restrictions involved. Here, again, we cannot repeat that massive information and would urge our readers to consult these and the following sources.

In addition, in 1935 Trnka published for British English an enormously detailed study of the relations of *every* consonant to *every* vowel in *every* monosyllabic morpheme of a list of over three thousand words, with the words themselves added for the monosyllables (and, in the first edition but not the second, for polysyllables). For example, (1966 edition: 36-7) he lists just which vowel phonemes do not occur before which consonants, and after which consonants; (ibid: 38-9) which consonants do and do not occur before and after which vowels; (ibid: 39-42), which consonants do and do not occur before and after others—with still further criteria and lists. His lists of most interest to us (ibid: 64-138) involve monomorphemic words of types VC (67 words), CV (175 words), CVC (1,346 words), VCC (30 words), CCV (124 words), CVCC (445 words), CCVC (714 words), CCCV (19 words), CVCCC (14 words), CCVCC (169 words), CCCVC (75 words), CCVCCC (3 words), CCCVCC (11 words)—with all these words illustrated with examples. In addition, he summarizes the results (with just one illustration for each pattern) for 2,221 further words of types VCV, VCVC, CVCV, . . . CCVCCCVCC. In order for the reader here to have a general idea of the kind of data available, an adaptation (in

symbols and arrangement) of one of his charts is given in Display
2.14, to represent his pattern CC(VC)—i.e. to show initial clusters
of two consonants in syllables closed with a single consonant.

Display 2.14 A Chart of Two Initial Consonants in Monomorphemic CCVC
Syllables of British English. Adapted from Trnka ([1935] 1966: 93); representing 714 words. The three groups of sounds enclosed in lines each represent
separate emic patterns (with gaps involving alloclasses), according to my analysis
as applied to his data as rearranged and marked for groupings here.

	l	r	w	y	m	n	p	t	k
p	21	23	−	3					
t	−	36	15	4					
k	41	41	25	2					
b	29	46	−						
d		29	3	6					
g	22	46							
f	32	21	−	5					
θ		14	2						
s	42	−	31	1	19	21	35	44	35
š		10							
m			−	3					
n				2					
l				4					
h				1					

A careful study of this chart (for which rows and columns have
been rearranged and hyphens and rectangular marks for the groups
have been added) will illustrate some of the problems of determining
the emic patterns involved. Note, first, the very sharp distributional
difference between /s/ and its following set of consonants, versus all
other material on the chart. This led us, in relation to the consonants
coming within the premargin tagmeme of Display 2.12, to treat /s/

and /š/ as comprising a special class of phonemes: the /š/ is in complementary distribution with /s/, occuring only with /r/, whereas the /s/, homorganic to /r/, does not occur there. The class is symbolized as c_3 in the emic pattern $\{c_3C_1\}$. This /s/ was analyzed as marginal to the cluster, since it is lower in rank than some of the consonants which follow it—i.e. the voiceless stops (see (f) for rank above). This judgement of C_1 as nuclear is confirmed by the large size of the set, which includes /l, r, w, y, m, n, p, t, k/ (see (e)). Note 'slip,' 'swing,' (suit), 'smooth,' 'snow,' 'spike,' 'stick' (Line 13), 'skill,' and 'shrine.' These two factors were used to override the counter evidence, that the /s/ is in some instances of higher rank, i.e. when the following consonant is /l, r, w, y, m, n/.

Yet even further confirmation of such a judgement is reached when one studies emic class $\{c_3C_4c_2\}$. There the set C_4 is exclusively /p, t, k/, and clearly nuclear to the cluster since it is of higher rank than either its premarginal /s/ (c_3) or its postmarginal /l, r, w, y/ (c_2) as seen in 'splash,' 'split,' 'street' (Line 4), (stupe), 'scram,' 'squeal.' Here, however, the c_3 alloclass includes /s/ only, not /s/ as well.

By analogy with the treatment of $\{c_3C_1\}$, there was postulated the small emic pattern $\{C_5c_6\}$,with C_5 as nuclear. Here C_5 is the larger of the two sets, made up of /m, n, l, h/, whereas c_6 is made up exclusively of /y/. Note 'mute,' (new), (lute), 'huge.'

This allows us to turn to the remaining data from Display 2.14 —the bulk of the chart—represented by the emic pattern $\{C_1(c_2)\}$. The first consonant is nuclear, since it is clearly of higher rank, composed of voiceless and voiced stops /p, t, k, b, d, g/ plus the far-front labial and interdental voiceless fricatives /f, θ/. The second consonant is marginal, made up of the lower-ranking liquids.

This, then, leaves the remaining data from Display 2.14—the bulk of the chart—as somewhat symmetrical, and suggests that in the basic emic pattern of $\{C_1(c_2)\}$ the first consonant is nuclear, since it is clearly of higher rank, composed of voiced and voiceless stops, the far-front labial and interdental voiceless fricatives /f, θ/, and is obligatory. The second is marginal but optional (as shown by the parentheses) and is made up of the lower-ranking liquids and semi-vowels /l, r, w, y/. Some gaps are symmetrical in relation to articulatory features—the homorganic gaps for labial not followed by labial, for example. Some of the examples given may be more British than American; if they do not fit our dialect, they are in parentheses: 'plate,' 'price,' 'puke,' 'treat,' 'twine,' (tune), 'clap,' 'cream,' 'quick,' 'cute,' 'black' (Line 19), 'broke,' 'dread,' 'dwell,' (duke), 'gloat,' 'green,' 'float,' 'from' (Line 10), 'fume,' 'throat,' thwack.'

Some readers may find help in understanding this kind of analysis from a suggestion made by Evelyn Pike comparing the problem of analyzing the immediate constituents of the syllable to that of the noun phrase. (See in Pike and Pike (1977: 51-54) the extensive chart of count noun phrases after Fries (1970), and the list of criteria for nucleus versus margin in grammatical matters, (ibid: 26-27), where independence of a class, ability to stand alone, large class, larger number of slots in which it occurs, and central semantic role lead to nuclearity in grammar.) Notice, for example, the handling of $\{c_3C_4c_2\}$ with 'my very big Tom' where 'Tom' is relatively independent in distribution (cf. 'Tom came,' as well as 'my big Tom came'). It also has a larger membership in its class of personal nouns (many names of people) than does the list of pronouns, of adverbs, or even of adjectives. There is layering of constituents, since 'very' modifies 'big' which could be shown by lower and upper case as 'very BIG,' with that phrase included in the whole noun phrase '[my (very big)] TOM' with bracketed and parenthetical items as optional, but with nuclear 'Tom' as obligatory.

An analysis similar to that for the premarginal consonants needs to be made for the postmarginal consonants. Yet this is difficult, for two reasons. First, there are morpheme borders within the syllable, and the desire to give this consideration by (b) above clashes with the place of occurrence of consonants of higher rank (see (f) above); and more than one high-ranking consonant may be found either within the monomorphemic part, or across morpheme boundaries. Compare, for example, the alternatives for 'looked' (Line 1), with high rank for both the /k/ and the suffix /t/, but with morpheme boundary between. There is a further complication: /t/ is given slightly higher ranking, as being more front in the mouth than the /k/ in the references quoted earlier.

Bloomfield (1933: 132) gave morphological criteria top priority by labelling as 'final' the last consonant of the stem morpheme in 'bet,' 'test,' and 'text.' The added phoneme in 'bets,' 'tests,' and 'texts,' he called 'post-final.' Then the /s/ of 'test' and of 'text' (/kst/) was 'pre-final,' with the /k/ of 'text' as 'second pre-final.' This labelling is awkward to maintain, when homophonous clusters can occur within one morpheme or be split between two. Compare the /kst/ of 'text' with the same clusters in 'axed'; or the /ks/ of 'six' with 'sicks' (of the present of 'to sick a dog on someone). Compare, also 'lapse' with 'lap-s;' 'tax' with 'tack-s;' 'quartz' with 'quart-s.'

One alternative seems to be to deal more directly with ranking, here, as we did in the premargin of the syllable. Then we have—as in Display 2.12—at least one cluster type with a high-ranking consonant at its beginning, shown by $\{C_R(c) \ldots\}$. In that symbolization, the R means 'high ranking;' and the dots mean 'with an unspecified number of marginal consonants following it.' This emic pattern would include, for example, the final clusters in 'looked' (Line 1), 'fix,' 'picks,' 'apt,' 'adze,' 'sixths.' The tentative contrastive pattern, for study, would then be the $\{c \ldots C_R \ldots\}$, with initial lower-ranking consonant. Compare 'lisps,' 'lisped,' 'pinched,' 'guest,' 'guessed,' 'vents,' 'penned,' 'clamped,' 'prompts,' 'glimpsed,' 'sphinx,' 'jinxed,' 'cold' (Line 6), 'pulp' (Line 11), 'raised' (Line 13), 'and' (Line 1).

2.11 SOME REMAINING PROBLEMS

Various other problems need to be studied before such a task as the one tackled in this article can be complete. For example, what should be done on the level of syllable contrast, and in relation to rhythm-group contrasts, with the classical handling of syllables with secondary stress? Compare 'grándsòn' with 'Jóhnson' (an illustration given by Eunice Pike—and always in the authors' dialect—contrastive). For some purposes we would prefer to treat this difference not as one of secondary stress, but rather as of *controlled* (or long) versus *ballistic* syllable type. See Pike (1967: 366-70) for discussion for English; and see Eunice Pike (1976) for its relevance to various other languages.

There is another problem: how are allophones of phonemes to be related to conditioning by rhythm groups? And how are rhythm groups to be—in part—reciprocally described in terms of allophones (as the aspiration of /p/ in English 'paper' helps locate the stress and describe the total phonological word, but placement in the second syllable of it conditions the lack of aspiration of the second occurrence of /p/)? For illustrations from a wide variety of languages, of the interlocking of levels in theory and practice, beyond the scope of English or this discussion, see Eunice Pike (1946). For discussion of an earlier stage of the theoretical problem, with interlocking levels, and extensive bibliography, see Pike (1976: 364-423). Many of the problems raised in 1955, are still waiting for wider discussion.

Perhaps, also, it is worth mentioning that much of the discussion in 1976 was focused on the specific units themselves, defined in terms of *feature* mode (*contrast*), *manifestation* mode (*variation* and physical content), and *distribution* mode. This is still highly useful —and often best employed—when one wishes to focus on a particular unit from the perspective of the fact that this *one unit* may occur in *various places* (in various units). When, however, one wishes to focus on the fact that some *one place* (slot) may be filled by several *different units*, the tagmemic formulas are often more useful.

Special styles may force, temporarily, special arrangements of constituents in relation to nucleus and margin. Just as, earlier in the chapter, we saw that the poetic *line* led to a special segmental analysis, for that poem, so here, at the level of the syllable, over differentiation may force a special analysis of the immediate constituents of that syllable. That is, the normal split of a syllable into immediate constituents in the form of a *string* (i.e. into C-V-C) may have to be supplemented, not replaced, by a hierarchically restructured C-VC arrangement; here the *VC* as a whole serves as the *riming* element, e.g. the '-ead' of both 'head' and 'dead' (Lines 5–6). Simultaneously with the normal string structuring, there can be the special riming structuring. And this, in turn, has implications of more widespread relevance: for various languages of Asia, it would seem that scholars for years have found it helpful to treat the vowel-plus-following-consonant as an appropriate section of the syllable; it may serve as a matrix for tonal distribution, for example.

Dialect differences, also, may affect the possibility of rime. In Lines 16–17 the author and the reader of the poem would seem to pronounce '-an' not only in 'man' but also in the riming 'understan(d).' A different, criss-crossing figure would be needed to diagram this larger composite constituent.

In other kinds of poetic lines, on the other hand, it would be the premargin consonant or consonant complex which would determine the tie of segments together phonetically; this is what happens in *alliteration*. In old English, for example, a line could have two parts, with two stresses to each part, and the parts joined by alliteration of the first three stressed syllables. See Pike (1945: 180). This would require further figures, somewhat like Display 2.7, breaking down the line (not the subparagraph) into halves, with the halves in turn broken into halves, and with cohesion (Cell 4) shown by the alliteration.

Internal to a line, in other poetic types, the repetition of a vowel (e.g. /o/) may carry qualitative impact (e.g. that of bigness or solemnity). In Chinese poetry a much more complicated pattern is sometimes seen: within a certain line (of a four-line poem) certain syllables must carry the same tone; others must avoid that tone; others may use either; and certain lines must end not only in a rime in tone, but also in a riming final vowel and consonant as well. See Pike (1948: 55).

In all of these types of syllables which involve calculated repetition of features, the tie of syllable to syllable, phonological word to phonological word, or line to line, needs to be shown. In tagmemic notation, this is done in the cohesion cells of the upper-level units (e.g. lines) so related, and in the lower-level unit (e.g. syllables, syllable nuclei, or syllable premargins) which force aesthetic attention to their relationship as phonological forms, or as semantically-related lexical elements.

2.12 CONCLUSION

Perhaps an approach such as the one given here can point toward a broader view in which the descriptive needs of widely different languages can be viewed within a single theoretical perspective. The *paradigmatic* (substitution class) relationships are represented directly either in the class cell of the tagmeme, or in lower-level breakdown formulas, or in the emic constructions seen within those cells. The *syntagmatic* features, on the other hand, show up in the breakdown formulas themselves, where the included parts of a unit are displayed in sequence. Within the slot cell of such an included tagmeme the syntagmatic features of nuclear versus marginal position are displayed. The cohesion cell, as we have just seen, relates various features of one unit to another in special ways while normal attention is given to optional versus obligatory occurrence, or to allo-constraints on the members of classes. And in the role cell, the relevance of the units displayed may be seen—contrastive differentiation as normal and basic, but occasionally with the intent to cause rime or other aesthetic effects.

3 The Tetrahedron as a Model for the Four-Cell Tagmeme in its Multiple Relations

Kenneth L. Pike

3.1 PROBLEMS IN LABELING THE ROWS AND COLUMNS OF THE FOUR-CELL TAGMEME MATRIX

The four-cell matrix (Pike and Pike 1977/1982: Chapters 3 and 12) has developed over a considerable period of time as a component of tagmemic theory. It has proved extremely useful for some time, both in our field work and in our theoretical development. In spite of this double advantage, which gave assurance that some component of truth was being captured, curious problems arose in labeling the rows and columns (vectors) of the two-by-two matrix representing the tagmeme. Before discussing these problems, and the kind of solution we are now proposing, a historical survey will be given of the way in which some components of the tagmeme came into view.

3.1.1 The 1954 two-cell tagmeme

In the first publication on tagmemics as such (see Pike 1954, or 1967: Section 7.742), the notation used only two components—*spot* (now *slot*) and filler *class*. A typical filler class of items would be a listing of items which could come in a particular grammatical slot (position). A noun phrase (one of various varieties) could come, for example, in a subject slot. Yet at the very beginning of tagmemic theory it was clear that this was insufficient to represent the data. One also had to know, for a transitive clause, for example, whether the subject was an actor in the clause, or an undergoer of the action (in active versus passive clauses). From the beginning, therefore, we spoke of things such as actor as subject, versus goal as subject (1954/ 1967: Sections 7.3, 7.321, 7.43), in an active versus a passive clause. Thus there was no single subject tagmeme for English, but a class of subject tagmemes, including actor as subject, versus goal (undergoer, patient) as subject, and others.

3.1.2 Development of the four-cell approach

As the importance of the distinction between actor versus goal as subject became more and more clear, we split those two in the notation, as well as in the analysis. This led to three cells—slot, class, and role—in the charting of the tagmeme, with earlier slot now split into slot and role.

This left an asymmetry which was not appealing. Becker tried a four-cell approach, with slot and class in an upper row of a two-by-two matrix, and role and category in the lower row of that matrix. He developed this (1967: 6) in a discussion of the English subject tagmeme. Becker used two rows to separate form from meaning and two columns to separate grammar from lexicon. (See Display 3.1). This captured not only the tagmeme as correlating syntactic slot and lexical filler, but also the idea of a form-meaning composite which was likewise postulated by the theory. He also gave (ibid: 16–46) extensive discussion of the relation of this material to work of Jespersen, Fries, Nida, transformational-generative grammar, and Fillmore, as well as (ibid: 47–77) Longacre.

Display 3.1 The Four-Cell Tagmeme as seen in Becker (1967: 14). Slot, filler class, role, and category are implicit in the cells of his chart. Rows contrast by form and meaning, and columns by grammar and lexicon. Cell B, for example, is 'lexical form.'

	Grammar	Lexicon
Form	A (e.g., Subject)	B (e.g., Noun Phrase)
Meaning	C (e.g., agent)	D (e.g., single, male, human, etc.)

Becker (ibid: 153) considered grammatical form to be surface structure and grammatical meaning to be deep structure. In this fourth cell, semantic categories such as single, male, etc. were given.

Wise (1968/1971: 24) suggested that the rows could be labeled as grammatical unit and lexemic unit instead of as form and meaning, and that the columns could be labeled as function versus manifestation. (See Display 3.2) Wise thought that this made it easier to handle discourse structure when the chronological order of the deep structure did not match the surface order, and made it easier to handle tagmemics as a whole.

Display 3.2 The Four-Cell Tagmeme as seen in Wise (1968/1971: 24). Rows contrast by grammatical unit versus lexemic unit, and columns by function and manifestation. The cells themselves are as in Becker (1967). Lexemic, here, does not mean lexical, but is closer to the term referential as used in Pike and Pike (1977/1982).

	Function	Manifestation
Grammatical Unit	A (e.g., Subject)	C (e.g., Noun Phrase)
Lexemic Unit	B (e.g., agent)	D (e.g. single, male, human, etc.)

Wise pointed out, for example, that Crawford (1963) applied the tagmeme more explicitly to phonology, while Wise was trying to apply the tagmeme to lexical-tagmeme material (1971: 25). It is important to notice in this connection, however, that lexemic here does not mean lexical. Lexical relates to *specific* lexical and dictionary entries but includes higher levels of idiom and the like, whereas her lexemic material is closer to what Pike and Pike (1977/1982) have called referential hierarchy. A further utilization of the four-cell tagmeme of the Becker type is found in Platt (1970/1971: 5), where he discussed the relation of tagmemic role to Fillmore's case grammar. At the same time Heidi Platt (1970) applied this concept to German as well as English. She treated the fourth cell as referring to the meaning component of the filler (1970: 17); the meaning of an item was split up into various semantic features, some more central than others.

But a problem had already begun to arise in the comparison of Wise's choice of lexical labels with those of Becker. Specifically, although they were in agreement on the elements within the cells of their matrices, they differed as to the labels. This implied that it was not a simple matter to define the relationships between the components of the rows and columns.

3.1.3 An interim nine-cell approach

It was then decided to try an integration of this four-cell grammatical tagmeme with materials from phonology and from specific lexical items. A nine-cell array (1974: 275) was set up. (See Display 3.3).

Display 3.3 The Interim Nine-Cell Approach preserved the contents of the upper left four cells intact, but with function, for the first column, and category or construction for the second column, and specific item as a third (instead of class of items). Phonology is added as a third row.

	Functional Slot, or Role	Category or Construction	Specific Item or Instance
Grammatical	1 e.g., subject	2 e.g., noun phrase	3 e.g., the boy
Sememic or Situational	4 e.g., actor	5 e.g., animate	6 e.g., Ted, son of Mr. Joe James of 420 Sixth Street
Phonological	7 e.g., ...	8 e.g., CV CVV	9 e.g., /ðə boʹ/

Notice that the content of the four cells in the upper left-hand corner is the same as for the comparable cells in Displays 3.1 and 3.2. The label of the second column, however, changes: *construction* is the term used to cover the set of members of a kind of class as filler of a slot, but *category* is added to cover more directly the nature of abstract features of meaning (second row) and of the phonology added by the third row. The specific item or instance is added as a third column, to make it possible to discuss directly the *particulars* of a situation rather than *general* rules or structures only. This opens the door to paraphrases of a particular item (either 'Ted' or 'The son of Joe James') as different ways of mentioning the same *encyclopedic* item, leading toward the Pike and Pike (1977/ 1982) referential hierarchy. At the same time, it points to the necessity of treating elements which control others in the context grammatically (e.g. singular to singular or subject to predicate), and in terms of truth value (with two plus three equalling seven, as false). Such constraints are related to a particular universe of discourse (with two plus two equalling one, truly, in the universe of discourse around a 'clock' face of zero, one, and two).

This display is advantageous in that it leaves room for much more data and further important relationships. But at the same time it involves serious problems. The phonological row (with its three cells) for example, does not give a chance to differentiate the four types of elements which were earlier handled for grammar in Display 3.1.

3.1.4 Four cells in all levels of three hierarchies

From this, therefore, a further matrix change was attempted by Pike and Pike (1977/1982). There a major decision was made to return to the four-cell tagmeme for grammar, but to add four-cell notations for phonology and reference separately. That would take care of the complexity needed for phonology and semantics by having separate hierarchies for them—and to each of these three hierarchies the four-cell tagmeme would be applied, at each level of these hierarchies. This had the great advantage that the same set of tagmemic concepts would be applied repeatedly, to each of the hierarchies and at each of the levels.

For example, in the phonology at the level of syllable, a class of CV syllables would fill its Cell 2; in the grammar at the level of phrase, a set of count-noun phrases would still be in Cell 2, as before; and in the referential hierarchy at the level of thing (or item or identity) the various paraphrases for 'Ted son of Joe James' would appear in its Cell 2. Thus we could treat very great interlocking empirical complexities of relationships across hierarchies and their levels with a more simple set of conceptual tools. It is not appropriate to discuss here the specific levels involved in these hierarchies (for grammar and reference see Pike and Pike (1977/1982), and Jones (1977); for phonology, see Chapter 2, in this volume) where riming relations comprise part of the controlling tie.

In addition, the 1974 nine-cell material (used in a more extensive but unpublished mimeographed form for classes in 1970) with its insistence on universe of discourse for truth relations, and with notational additions for relevant settings, suggested the need for a broader term for Cell 4 of Display 3.1.

But a further change was involved in this reworking. Lexical material, instead of itself comprising the hierarchy (as it was in Pike (1967: Sections 10.2, 15.13), with a poem or a text as a top unit of the lexical hierarchy) *manifested all three* hierarchies, including the referential one. This did *not* mean a sharp separation of form (in one hierarchy) from meaning (as comprising another). Rather there was *meaning* postulated for *each unit* of *each* hierarchy, with meaning as speaker intent, or as hearer understanding, or as behavioral impact (Section 16). For example, the role of Cell 3 of the grammar was just one particular kind of meaning, that of grammatical role, or function. Many other things of importance are involved in this decision—for example the resultant treatment of the referential tagmemic structure of a particular member of a cast or of an event—but it is not appropriate to discuss them here. See, however, Chapter

12 in Pike and Pike (1982) and see Chapters 2 and 3 of this volume). It is important, however, to add here that each of these three hierarchies is manifested through lexical items, in a particular allostructure of any one utterance, from morpheme to text. (See Display 3.4).

Display 3.4 The Three Hierarchies of Reference, Grammar, and Phonology intersect in (share) the lexical manifesting substance; none of them is abstracted away from the substance. For Slot, one may ask where a particular structure fits as a constituent in an immediately larger including one; is it nuclear or marginal to that structure viewed as wave? For Class, one wishes to know what item or set of items is substitutable in that slot; is it audible, visible, concrete? For Role, one wishes to know what the relevance of the item is to the structure or situation; why is the event taking place, or by what intent, or with what structural meaning? For Cohesion, one wishes to know what controls this item, or what it is controlling; is it in agreement with some other, and is it part of an underlying larger system that determines the relevance of this area?

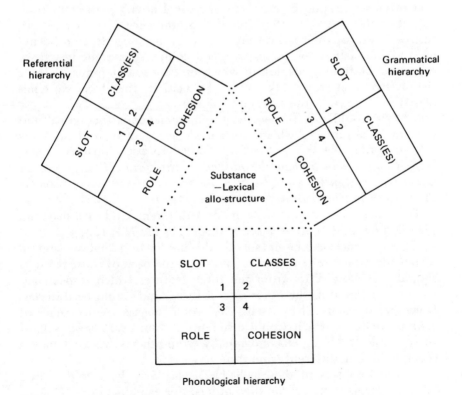

Phonological hierarchy

3.2 A PROBLEM IN OVERLAPPING ROWS AND COLUMNS

Next we studied the labels of the rows and columns of the revised four-cell tagmeme for the three hierarchies. But we had great difficulty labeling the rows and columns of the two-by-two matrix so that they would be consistent.

We found that we had been working on an assumption which we did not recognize was there until much later: *We were assuming that the features labeling the rows would be mutually exclusive; and that when there are only two rows, one would somehow be 'plus' that feature and the other 'minus;' and that this would lead to a symmetry in the matrix.* This implied that there should be *no overlap* of the contrasting features between the two rows, since if there were such an overlap, the exclusiveness of the component implied by the labels would be destroyed, and the symmetry would be lost.

Yet this was precisely the difficulty we ran into, if one row were labeled form, and the other row labeled meaning. Meaning of some kind was clearly present in the second row (in role), but there was also often a meaning of class (e.g. personal noun) in the first row; and even the slot cell often included prominence (focus) which in turn we were treating as a variety of impact meaning. So after having used various labels for these rows and columns for some years, we despaired of finding a solution which met those requirements for a two-by-two matrix. In Pike and Pike (1977), therefore, we eliminated the names for the rows and columns.

Yet we could not throw away the tremendous theoretical and procedural advantages which we had already gained from the four-cell structure. We were, therefore, forced to ask a different question: *Could there perhaps be hidden in this four-cell structure an underlying system of a kind which we had never noticed or thought of or seen described? And if so how could we represent it?*

To answer this question, we made a different kind of a diagram. (See Display 3.5) In it, each set of three cells (2, 3, 4; 1, 3, 4; 1, 2, 4; 1, 2, 3) is enclosed in lines with the implication that we should search for a feature common to each set. And each of those features should somehow differ from the three features which respectively were to be found in the other sets of three, and would be different from that of each cell by itself. This would suggest the existence of criterial features which would differentiate four *overlapping* sets of three, while the four cells *individually* would themselves each have a separate feature different from those.

Of the four sets of these cells in Display 3.5, the shared feature of some seems more certain than others. For example, in Set C (1, 2,

Display 3.5 Features Identifying the Four Cells, with a peculiar structure. Each cell by itself has such a feature. In addition, each set of three shares a further feature. This implies a total structure quite different from an ordinary two-times-two matrix where one feature would be plus-present for one row, but minus-present for the other (and, comparably, for columns).

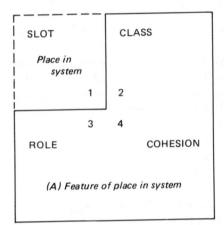

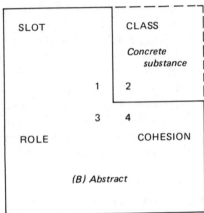

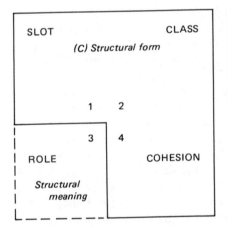

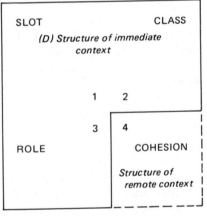

4—slot, class, cohesion) the three linked cells all seem to be reflecting elements of *formal* structure (as over against the *informal* role of Cell 3); in addition, however, each of these can be differentiated, such that class seems to reflect *particle*; cohesion seems to reflect *field*; and the slot, with its nuclear vs. marginal possibilities, seems to reflect *wave*.

Similarly, in Set D (1, 2, 3—slot, class, role) each cell seems to be referring to the structure of the *immediate context*. Slot implies a place in an immediately larger structure; class provides the item which is in fact filling that immediate context; and role refers to the function or relevance of that class of items to the containing immediate context.

This much, then, was immediately very encouraging. We wanted to check the other two sets, but these proved to be more difficult; it was harder to observe what the relationships were.

For Set A (2, 3, 4—class, role, cohesion), each reflects some underlying *feature* of a place in a local or larger system (whereas slot would itself *be* a place in the immediately including local system). For example, a class helps define where a place is; a role helps define what function that place has; and features of agreement, as one component of cohesion, tie together two or more slots in a system.

On the other hand, Set B (1, 3, 4—slot, role, cohesion) is *abstract*, as over against the concreteness of class; they are not visible or audible like the normal members of a class.

3.3 FROM MATRIX TO TETRAHEDRON WITH EACH FACE 'OPPOSITE' TO A POINT

A first clue to understanding this shape of structure was given by the mathematician John Upton of Australia. He showed that we might be needing to work with pairs of two cells, including both those which were horizontal and those which were vertical in the matrix, and *in addition* with the two *diagonal* pairs of cells. These latter sets we had not worked with directly, although we had been puzzled by them, since the arrangement of the four cells in rows and columns continued to be valid even if instead of placing them as rows 1, 2, and 3, 4, one made the rows 1, 3, and 2, 4. In addition, he showed that one could take each of the resultant six pairs and by overlapping them make a further matrix which would describe much of the data. At the time, however, we were unable to get structural insight from this suggestion, although later part of it proved to be important, as we shall see below.

The next stage came several months later. Fred Lupke, a graduate student at the University of Michigan, suggested that a *tetrahedron* might be a useful model. (A tetrahedron can be thought of as a pyramid with a triangular base which counts as one of its four faces; rotating the pyramid appropriately can bring the base into the place of one of the other three faces.) This later became the crucial breakthrough suggestion. Paul Keogh, another student, suggested entering the names for the cells at the four corners (vertices) of the tetrahedron, and Howard McKaughn, a Professor of Linguistics from the University of Hawaii, suggested entering the names for the cells on the *faces* of the tetrahedron. Both give equivalent initial results (but see below, Postscript, Section 3.7), utilizing the same data and preserving all of the same contrasts; the 'translation' from the one to the other, however, was not easy to visualize before we actually went through the graphing of the material. We personally preferred to put the cell *content* on the *faces* of the tetrahedron (see Display 3.6), reserving the points for the shared features of those cells. Mathematicians, however, might for some purposes prefer to give the vertices prominence, by placing the cell material there, since they easily deal with abstract points and lines, whereas we prefer a place—or space— to enter names of concrete data such as words or manifested structures.

Display 3.6 A View of a Tetrahedron from the Top. The three visible faces appear to meet in the centered point. A fourth face is invisible, underneath the pyramid; rotating the upper point to the ground position would bring the fourth face into view. The faces are labelled and numbered according to the cells in any one of the three areas of Display 3.4. The currently hidden cell is labelled with an arrow to show that the label applies to the face on the ground.

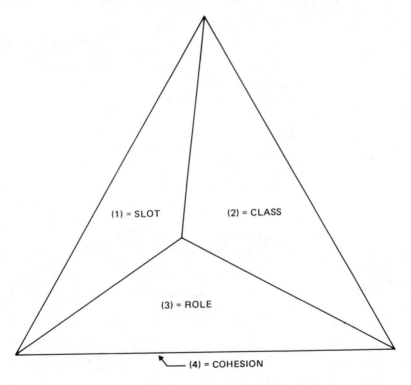

(1) = SLOT

(2) = CLASS

(3) = ROLE

(4) = COHESION

If the tetrahedron is held between the fingers so that a point is touched by one finger, and a face by the thumb, then the tetrahedron can be rotated around that axis between the two. That is, the face is *opposite* to the *point*—as mathematician-linguist Ivan Lowe has pointed out. See, therefore, in Display 3.7 that the faces

Display 3.7 The Tetrahedron, with the Number and Name of Each Cell on One Face. In addition, to each cell is added the general characteristic which differentiates it more generally from the composite features of the remaining three cells. The feature shared by a set of three cells which contrasts it with such an opposite face cell is seen at one of the points labelled A, B, C, or D. Thus, for point versus face:

(A) = (2, 3, 4), vs. (1);   (C) = (1, 2, 4), vs. (3);
(B) = (1, 3, 4), vs. (2);   (D) = (1, 2, 3), vs. (4);

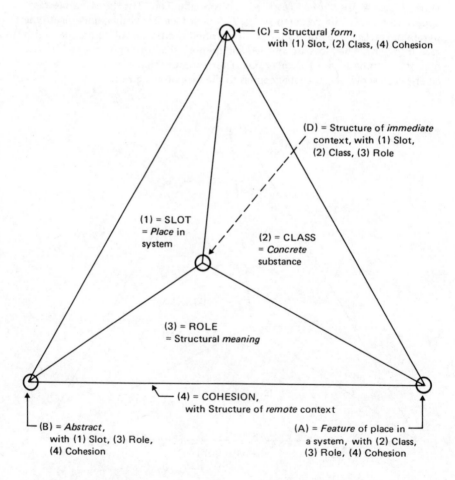

(C) = Structural *form*, with (1) Slot, (2) Class, (4) Cohesion

(D) = Structure of *immediate* context, with (1) Slot, (2) Class, (3) Role

(1) = SLOT = *Place* in system

(2) = CLASS = *Concrete* substance

(3) = ROLE = Structural *meaning*

(4) = COHESION, with Structure of *remote* context

(B) = *Abstract*, with (1) Slot, (3) Role, (4) Cohesion

(A) = *Feature* of place in a system, with (2) Class, (3) Role, (4) Cohesion are labeled with the names of the cells (as slot, class, role, and cohesion) and their isolated, distinctive features, while the points are labeled with those features seen in Display 3.5 which unite three cells (faces in Display 3.7). That is, each *point (vertex) is the meeting place of a feature shared by three faces*; and each face has a further feature distinct from these and from each other. The isolated feature of the one cell by itself is the opposite, in the sense used here, of the feature shared by the other three cells. Thus, in Display 3.7, the feature of structural meaning, of the face (3) role, is the opposite of the feature of structural form, of the point (c).

Basically this broke the back of the problem. We had found a model which seemed to 'make sense' of the queerness of cells grouped by overlapping threes sharing a feature. That is, *we were dealing with a different kind of n-dimensional space from that represented by a two-dimensional matrix*—or by a three-dimensional one which *merely* expanded the regular binary contrasts in number but not in basic kind of plus-minus interrelations. What we had needed was *not more dimensions* in the ordinary regular, binary sense, but a more elaborate kind of relationship which the tetrahedron helped us to see.

Structural meaning (3), for example, is not merely the absence of structural form (1, 2, 4), nor is structural form merely the absence of structural meaning. Both form *and* meaning are *positive* occurring components. Similarly, place in a system (1) is not quite either the absence or the presence of a feature of such a place. On the other hand, we eventually came up with labels of *remoteness* for (4) versus *immediacy* for (1, 2, 3) which sound more like a classical plus-minus pair, as do *concrete* for (2) versus *abstract* for (1, 3, 4). But such pairings, which sound rather clean cut now, were by no means obvious; the tetrahedron pattern forced us to look for such pairings, some of which might have otherwise escaped our attention for a very long time. 'Obvious' in retrospect is not the same as obvious at the time. And once the model has been given more attention, it is quite possible that even better labels will be found, if our mental search pattern has been loosened up in this way.

3.4 OPPOSITE EDGES ON THE TETRAHEDRON

But now a further question arose: Did the *edges* of the tetrahedron have any mappable relationship to the data which we had been working with? There were six such edges—but we had not been working with any explicit naming of six units. Could the model be forcing our attention to something here that we had been over-looking?

This made us look again at Upton's and Lupke's suggestion about the six relationships between the four cells in Displays 3.1 and 3.2 —horizontal, vertical and diagonal.

But a still further observation about the tetrahedron was brought to our attention by Lowe. He pointed out that there are also *opposite edges* in the tetrahedron—with opposite defined in a special way which we had not known. That is, a certain 'horizontal' edge—lying flat, say, at the front base of the pyramid—had no corner which it shared with the slanting 'upright' edge at the back of the pyramid. These two edges were opposite—in balanced symmetry in that special sense—*not parallel* but at right angles to each other, although not meeting or crossing. This, again, suggested a highly different definition of contrasts from our earlier implicit assumption about contrasting symmetries in a matrix. Here, also, opposite *did not necessarily mean that a feature was plus in one row but minus in another.* Rather it meant that there were features which were not shared although related in some sense by certain relationally-defined parts of the system.

We sought, therefore, for a feature which would be shared by class and cohesion (2, 4), but not by slot and role (1, 3); and for a feature shared by slot and role but not by class and cohesion, yet with the two pairs in some kind of general (or, at the moment, vague) paralleling relationship. Note, then, on Display 3.8 that the edge (1, 3) suggests that both slot and role are in some sense relating the tagmeme to its environment *syntagmatically* whereas the opposite but nonparallel edge (2, 4) suggests that both class and cohesion are related to their environment in a more paradigmatic way. Similarly, edge (1, 2) suggests that slot and class can be *overtly* studied, in relation to the construction under narrow immediate attention, whereas the opposite edge (3, 4) implies that the data of role and cohesion may be somewhat *covert*, in the sense that they must be deduced from sociolinguistic or psychological environment (role), or from the background belief system or larger agreement (cohesion). Edge (2, 3) suggests that it may be relatively *easy* to make a student *aware* of class and role, whereas edge (1, 4) implies that it may prove more *difficult* to make the student aware of slot and cohesion. (Here, however, as in relation to labels for the points in Display 3.7 better descriptive terms may later be selected while staying within the confines of the model.)

If, now, one compares Display 3.7 with Display 3.8 one sees that it is important to check to see that the labels for the points of

Display 3.8 The Edges of the Tetrahedron Shared by Two Cells; the specific edge is labeled according to the number-name of the shared cell pair. For example, (1, 4) means the edge shared by Slot and (the temporarily hidden) Cohesion; (1, 2) is shared by Slot and Class cells. Names on the edges are labels of features shared by the sharing cells; for example, (1, 3), Slot and Role, share some important syntagmatic relation to the items of the immediately larger context. These relationships are in addition to, simultaneously, those of the points labeled in Display 3.7.

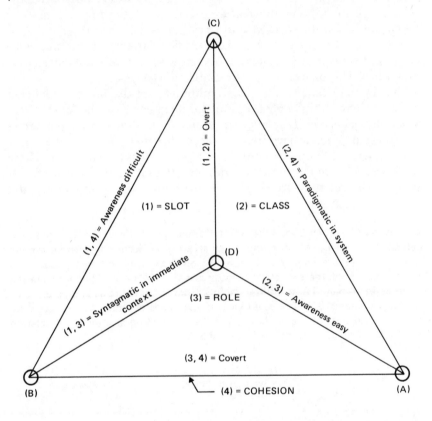

Display 3.7 are not the same as the labels for the edges of Display 3.8. This difference is crucial to the discussion. If the edges meant the same as the points, there would be a denial of the difference between a feature shared by two cells only, as over against a *different set* of features shared by three cells; and it was this latter characteristic which led to the problem under discussion, when we saw that a defining feature of row 2, say, of Displays 3.1 and 3.2 might be found also in one of the cells of row 1. The current analysis appears to have accounted for the three-cell groupings.

3.5 FEATURES OF THE FOUR-CELL TAGMEME MATRIX RELABELED

While we were working on Displays 3.7 and 3.8, we were also trying to rework the labels of the rows and columns of the four-cell matrix (cf. Displays 3.1 and 3.2). Did the labeling of Display 3.5, with its three-cell combinations, avoid the inconsistency ·of the earlier struggles? Did the labeling of the six edges of the tetrahedron now lead to perspicuity in the feature relations of the four-cell matrix, when applied both to rows and to columns, and to diagonals? And did the fact of the presence of six possible relations for the four cells, suggested by Upton (see Section 3.3) now seem reasonable instead of awkward? The answer to the three questions is yes.

See Display 3.9, where rows, columns, and diagonals are labeled as in Display 3.8. Compare, also, the differences in the labels there with the labels in Displays 3.1 and 3.2. For the rows, the terms *overt* versus *covert* have here replaced (for now, at least) the terms *form* versus *meaning*, or *grammatical unit* versus *lexemic unit*. These new terms are much more general, and at first sight not as useful. It is only in relation to the larger structure, and consistency, and

Display 3.9 Two-Cell Labels for Rows, Columns, and Diagonals. Here the two-cell labels for rows, columns, and diagonals are given according to those worked out in relation to the study of the tetrahedron as a model, with its six edges, and the suggestion of the six relations as discussed with Upton. The labels are the same as in Display 3.8, but differ sharply from those for rows and columns of Displays 3.1 and 3.2. The reworking of the labels attempts to represent my study growing out of the application of the tetrahedron as a model, in relation to its edges (versus its points, in Display 3.8).

	(1, 3) = Syntagmatic in immediate context	(2, 4) = Paradigmatic in system
(1, 4) = Awareness difficult		
(1, 2) = Overt	(1) = SLOT = Place in system	(2) = CLASS = Concrete substance
(3, 4) = Covert	(3) = ROLE = Structural meaning	(4) = COHESION = Structure of remote context
(2, 3) = Awareness easy		

especially in relation to implications and insights from the new model, that the difference is justified. Similarly, the difference between emphasis on *syntagmatic* (with reservation about immediate context) versus *paradigmatic* (without that reservation) is strikingly different. And the diagonal labeling of difficult versus easy awareness of slot and cohesion versus role and class is not reflected in the earlier figures.

In addition, a former puzzle is solved: Did it not sometimes seem helpful to put early analytical attention on class and role, before trying to deal with slot? And why did it at other times seem better to deal with slot and class before role? It would appear that 'rightness' was not involved. Rather there were six relations in the four-cell structure, not four; diagonal was as correct as row or column. Hence one could use the particular relation which seemed most appropriate for the task at hand, or for the starting insights available to the analyst of the moment, whether available to him because of historical accident or personal disposition. Diagonal role-with-class was as valid as row slot-with-class. A permutation of the matrix such that diagonal role-with-class would become a row of role-with-class left the system of relationships unchanged.

3.6 THE SIGNIFICANCE OF THE TETRAHEDRON MODEL FOR THE TAGMEME

What are some of the general principles which this experience with the tetrahedron suggest which might be helpful for future work in language and in nonverbal behavior?

(a) That which appears to be irregular from the perspective of a low hierarchical level may turn out in fact to be regular when seen from the broader perspective of a higher level of the hierarchy. A mathematical formalism may obtain its helpful appearance of regular rules at the cost of concealing exceptions; it needs a higher level mathematics to correct this—and if that is not available then informal devices must be used to treat the data. As Vern Poythress said: 'The problem is that when you start working with a mathematical model the immediate tendency is to get things which will work to a first order but will not take care of the second order problems (irregularities), and in a sense make the second order problems worse because the tendency is to just ignore them since you can no longer deal with them in the formalism you set up.'

(b) The most useful selection of contrastive features is not necessarily the one which chooses those which merely signal the

presence versus the absence of some feature, but may rather sometimes be features which contrast vectors of a system by related
but positive content.

(c) The simplest formalism is not necessarily the most productive,
nor the most valid. As logician Langer (1953: 185) says, 'We are no
longer limited to propositions that are simple, obvious, and generally
entertained. If we chance upon a fairly complex and even surprising
proposition, from which very many simple ones would follow, we are
perfectly justified in taking the former as a postulate and deriving
the others from it.' We are assuming that something of this kind is
involved in the reworking of Displays 3.1 and 3.2 to Display 3.9
in the light of the work with the tetrahedron in Displays 3.6 and
3.8. A mathematical reductionism is not always desirable in linguistic
work. At times complexity is a more enlightening starting point:
phones are easier to record at the beginning of the study of a language
than are abstract phonetic features; and the choice of some characteristics of grammar inside a sentence may be intelligible only after
one studies them from the point of view of their inclusion in a text.

(d) The character of n-dimensional arrays is not determined by the
number of present-versus-absent features. Sometimes it represents
a radically different kind of relationship; a difference in kind of
dimension is not the same as an addition of a dimension. And
'opposite' may have different definitions in different dimension
systems.

(e) Since the four cells of the tagmeme can be arranged in different ways, their order appears to be immaterial. Different displays
of the same elements do not destroy the underlying system. (For
example, if one writes the data of Displays 3.7 and 3.8 on a paper
tetrahedron, and then slices open the visible edges, rewriting the
data on the inner surfaces of the now flat display, one may obtain
Display 3.10. In it the sliced former edges now appear as two half-
lengths of one side of the large triangle. But the former 'hidden'
cohesion face is now in the center of the display.)

(f) The tagmeme, seen in some of its complexity here, is given
support as a genuine unit of language system and not as a mere
arbitrary stopping place of description.

(g) Once the way into further complexity is opened up through
this particular door, one can more easily learn from other theories,
finding in them some of the data which needs to be incorporated
into any theory growing toward fuller description.

Display 3.10 The Tetrahedron 'Opened Up' and Relabeled. The formerly invisible cohesion cell is now in view at the center. With point D opened up, the edge (1, 2) is now split, and doubled—and given the repeated label, as overt. Slot and Class could be reversed in position, for example, with no change in the system, if the points show properly their shared features. Lowe points out the newly developed parallelisms between edges from opened-up points (e.g. 1, 2 = overt) and earlier edges (3, 4 = covert).

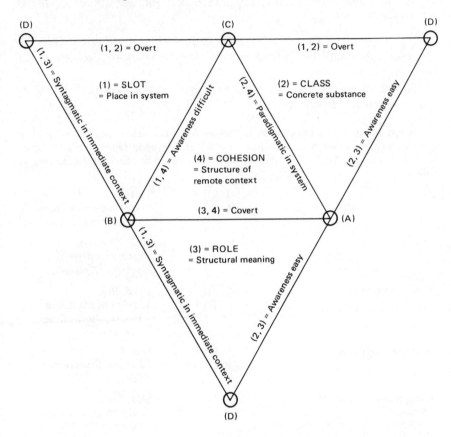

3.7 A POSTSCRIPT ON LIMITS OF FORMALISM

In Section 3.3 above we had discussed the fact that we had chosen to put the content of the cells on the faces of the tetrahedron, with the features on the points; and we mentioned that although we preferred that choice, mathematically the opposite choice could have been made. Upton expands on that fact: not only do the vertices contain the shared features on the adjoining faces, but there is a dual which is also worth observing, namely that, in addition, the faces (cells) contain the shared features of the adjoining vertices. Whether or not this observation has any linguistic value is beyond my judgement but I have drawn the dual of Display 3.7 (not shown here, KLP), in which the duals of the vertices A, B, C, D are the faces A', B', C', D', and the duals of the faces (1), (2), (3), (4), are the vertices (1'), (2'), (3'), (4'). Using the same pattern as in Display 3.7 it is then apparent that, say, the vertex (1') = SLOT has the shared features of the three cells (B') abstract, (C') Structural form, and (D') Structure of immediate context.

The diagram of this dual is fascinating—but we do not see that it changes the linguistic interpretation. We leave it to the reader to draw this dual.

On the other hand, Upton has a further suggestion which is not so easy to handle. He says:

A second observation, again with uncertain linguistic value, is that, in Display 3.8, the edges are not only common to pairs of adjoining faces (cells) but also, in a dual sense, to pairs of adjoining vertices. Thus each edge can be labeled as follows:

Overt	= (1, 2):	Slot, Class
	= (C, D):	Structural form, Immediate context.
Covert	= (3, 4):	Role, Cohesion
	= (A, B):	Feature of place in a system, Abstract.
Awareness easy	= (2, 3):	Class, Role
	= (A, D):	Feature of place in a system, Immediate context.
Awareness difficult	= (1, 4):	Slot, Cohesion
	= (B, C):	Abstract, Structural form.
Syntagmatic in immediate context	= (1, 3):	Slot, Role
	= (B, D):	Abstract, Immediate context.
Paradigmatic in System	= (2, 4):	Class, Cohesion
	= (A, C):	Feature of place in a system, Structural form.

And, again, he adds that it is not possible for him to assess the linguistic value of these observations. But whereas the first dual component, interchanging faces and points, makes little apparent difference to the linguistic description, the second phase of the dual operation is surprising. When one adds the labels of the edges of

Display 3.8 to the drawn edges of the dual of Display 3.8, those drawn edges no longer come between tagmemic cells (slot, class, role, and cohesion) directly, but between *features* of those elements (since the dual of the line-drawn edge is *no longer a line*, but a point). And the shared drawn-edge relation between any two cells of Display 3.8 is not, therefore, the same as the shared drawn-edge relation of the features shared by pairs of faces of the dual. But what is the implication of this? Probably that the contribution of this model has reached its easy limit. To push it further, by way of the dual, may not currently—if ever—be profitable. Or would it now be necessary to give new, further statements of the implied feature shared by two features adjacent to the newly-drawn edges of the dual?

And IF WE LEAVE IT UNTREATED, HOW DAMAGING IS IT? —either to this particular description, or to linguistic technology if similar residues are left untreated elsewhere? Robert Dooley suggests: that a model, including such a mathematical one as this, should be treated *as a metaphor*; that *all* metaphors must be utilized with care not to push them too far; that all metaphors can be pushed to where their detailed application is not relevant. See, for example, Chapter 1 of my *Linguistic Concepts* (1982). Nor does the usefulness of a metaphor demand total applicability. So, here, the tetrahedron has proved useful, but we do not need to insist that the application of its mathematical dual be carried further.

Dooley affirms that with all formalisms in linguistics we must beware of over-extending their apparent implications. A good formalism is a useful tool, but should not be allowed to grow into a tyrant. All metaphors, models, and theories are limited in applicability, and none should be pushed to the 'nothing but' break point. None— including tagmemics—should be allowed the claim that it fills or explains the *entire* universe. More remains to be done—and thought and learned.

And this viewpoint illustrates another attitude of ours. Our own ignorance is profound. Many phases of human knowledge we do not, can not, and never will control. It, however, we take our own material as a model-with-limits, it is not only useful to get help from mathematicians such as those we have mentioned, but a *delight*. And so with other phases of human knowledge. Just as tagmemics emphasizes the need to see data in context, so our approach is able to accept with appreciation the context of knowledge within which we all live, and *in relation to* which certain advances must be made if they are to be made at all.[1]

NOTE

1 When I mailed this postscript to Upton, he sent back the following encouraging reply:

The comments which you make and which you quote from Robert Dooley seem to me to be very pertinent. For a mathematical model is no more than a model and its characteristic is to display certain features of the entity of which it is a model. Other features of the entity may not be displayed by the model and some characteristics of the model may not relate to features of the entity. My comments to you were concerned with properties of the model different from those which enabled the model to be formed in the first instance. While it is possible that these further properties may have some linguistic value or while they may characterize other (possibly hitherto unsuspected) features of the entity, equally they may not have any linguistic value at all and I agree with Dooley that we must beware of over-extending apparent implications.

Work goes on. One insight suggests another. New formalisms urge new precisions. Insight and purpose are not enough. Rigor and checking are not by themselves inventors. Socialized observer and emicized thing overlap. Let us, also, grow in fusion of delight and understanding.

Bibliography

Becker, A. (1967), 'A Generative Description of the English Subject Tagmeme,' Ph. D. dissertation, Ann Arbor, University of Michigan.

Black, M. and Smalley, W. A. (eds), (1974), *Language, Culture, and Religion: in Honor of Eugene A. Nida*, The Hague, Mouton.

Bloomfield, L. (1933), *Language*, New York, Holt: London, Allen and Unwin, 1935.

Brend, R. M. and Pike, K. L. (eds), (1976), *Tagmemics*, The Hague, Mouton.

Brinkley, narrator (1965), 'The Funeral of Sir Winston Churchill,' London, January 30, 1965, with Excerpts from his Speeches, National Geographic Society and Decca Record Co., Ltd.

Crawford, (1963), *Totontepec Mixe Phonotagmemics*, Linguistic Series of the Summer Institute of Linguistics of the University of Oklahoma 8.

Erickson, C. J. and Pike, E. G. 'Semantic and Grammatical Structures in an Isirawa Narrative,' in Suharmo and Pike (1976: 63-93).

Foley, W. A. and Van Valin, D., Jr. (1977), 'On the Viability of the Notion of 'Subject' in Universal Grammar,' *Berkeley Linguistics Society* 3, 293-320.

Grimes, E. (1975), *The Thread of Discourse*, The Hague, Mouton.

Grimes, J. E. (ed) (1978), *Papers on Discourse*, Summer Institute of Linguistics, Publications in Linguistics 51. Dallas, Summer Institute of Linguistics and University of Texas at Arlington.

Halliday, A. K. and Hasan, R. (1976), *Cohesion in English*, London, Longman.

Jones, K. (1977), *Theme in English Expository Discourse*, Edward Sapir Monograph Series in Language, Culture, and Cognition 2, Lake Bluff, Jupiter Press.

Langer, K. (1953), 2nd ed, *An Introduction to Symbolic Logic*, New York, Dover Publications.

Longacre, E. (1981), *A Spectrum and Profile Approach to Discourse Analysis*, The Hague, Mouton, Text I, 4: 337-59.

Longacre, R. E. and Woods, F. (eds), (1976-7), *Discourse Grammar: Studies in Indigenous Languages of Columbia, Panama, and Ecuador, three parts*, Summer Institute of Linguistics, Publications in Linguistics 52, Dallas, Summer Institute of Linguistics and University of Texas at Arlington.

Martin, R. and Pike, L. (1974), 'Analysis of the Vocal Performance of a Poem: A Classification of Intonational Features,' *Language and Style*, 7, 209-18.

Miller, A. (1956) 'The Magical Number Seven, Plus or Minus Two: Some Limits on our Capacity for Information Processing,' *Psychological Review*, 63, 81-97.

Miller, G. A. and Johnson-Laird, P. N. (1976), *Language and Perception*. Cambridge, Harvard University Press.

Nida, A. (1975), *Componential Analysis of Meaning*, The Hague, Mouton.

Parisi, D. and Castelfranchi, C. (1976), *The Discourse as a Hierarchy of Goals*, Urbino, Centro Internazionale d'Semiotica di Linguistica, Extract: 12-36.

Pike, E. V. (1954), 'Phonetic Rank, and Subordination in Consonant Patterning and Historical Change, *Miscellanea Phonetica*, 2, 3-41.

Pike, E. V. (1976), 'Phonology,' in Brend and Pike (1976: Vol. 1, 45–83).

Pike, K. L. (1945), *The Intonation of American English*, University of Michigan Publications in Linguistics 1, Ann Arbor, University of Michigan Press.

Pike, K. L. (1947), 'On the Phonemic Status of English Diphthongs,' *Language*, 23, 151–9.

Pike, K. L. and Pike, E. V. (1947), 'Immediate Constituents of Mazatec Syllables, *International Journal of American Linguistics* 13, 78–91.

Pike, K. L. (1948), *Tone Languages*, University of Michigan Publications in Linguistics 4, Ann Arbor, University of Michigan Press.

Pike, K. L. (1954, 1955, 1960 1st ed in three volumes, 1967, 2nd ed) *Language in Relation to a Unified Theory of the Structure of Human Behavior*, The Hague, Mouton.

Pike, K. L. (1963), 'The Hierarchical and Social Matrix of Suprasegmentals,' *Prac Filologicznych*, 18, 95–104.

Pike, K. L. (1966), 'On the Grammar of Intonation,' *Proceedings of the Fifth International Congress of Phonetic Sciences* 105–19, Basel, Karger.

Pike, K. L. 'Agreement Types Dispersed into a Nine-Cell Spectrum,' in Black and Smalley (1974: 175–86).

Pike, K. L. and Bernstein, J. 'The Emic Structure of Individuals in Relation to Dialogue,' in Van Dijk and Petöfi (1977: 1–10).

Pike, K. L. and Pike, E. G. (1977/1982, 2nd ed) *Grammatical Analysis*, Summer Institute of Linguistics, Publications in Linguistics 53, Dallas, Summer Institute of Linguistics.

Platt, H. K. L. (1970), 'A Comparative Study of England and German Syntax,' Ph. D. dissertation, Monash University.

Platt, J. T. (1970/1971), *Grammatical Form and Grammatical Meaning; a Tagmemic View of Fillmore's Deep Structure Case Concepts*, Amsterdam, North Holland.

Suharno, I. and Pike, K. L. (eds), (1976), *From Baudi to Indonesian*, Cenderawasih University and Summer Institute of Linguistics.

Trnka, B (1935/1966), *A Phonological Analysis of Present-day Standard English*, Revised edition, Kanekiyo, T. and Koizumi, T. (eds), University, Alabama, University of Alabama Press.

Van Dijk, T. A. (1977), *Text and Context: Exploration in the Semantics and Pragmatics of Discourse*, London, Longman.

Van Dijk, T. A. (1978), 'New Developments and Problems in Textlinguistics,' *AILA Bulletin*, No. 1 (22): 13–26.

Van Dijk, T. A. and Petöfi, J. S. (eds), (1977), *Grammars and Descriptions*, Berlin, Grupter.

Index

Educational Linguistics/TESOL/ICC
Graduate School of Education
University of Pennsylvania
3700 Walnut Street/C1
Philadelphia, PA   19104